# Praise for *Telugu Christians*

"The attraction of the message of the gospel to people who were not primarily intended to be its recipients, and the incredibly diverse communities that eventually came into existence under the capacious tent of Christianity fascinate anyone interested in the regional history of India. The manifold groupings of Telugu Christians described in this book trace their backgrounds to denominational traditions, Bhakti movements, and inspirational individuals. James Taneti has successfully captured this diversity even as he makes clear that the message of the gospel was readily accepted by communities that had no standing among the dominant segments of the contemporary society. By moving away from a singular focus on the history of a specific Christian denomination, Taneti commendably captures the broad history of the evolution of the different and yet overlapping Christian communities among the Telugu people."

—Mrinalini Sebastian, literary critic and research scholar,
Harcum College Partnership Site at Grace-Trinity UCC, Philadelphia

"James Taneti's *Telugu Christians* is a concise history which focuses on the Telugu Christian people and how they both spread and shaped Christianity in their part of India. He presents Christianity there as a product of the interactions between foreign missionary Christianity, dominant caste Hindu religion and culture, and the Dalit culture (with a strong feminine input) from which most Christians have been drawn. While emphasizing the Protestant experience there, the history is also ecumenical in scope and sensitive to parallel developments elsewhere in India. The history is well researched and well thought through. I definitely recommend it for publication."

—John C.B. Webster, professor of church history at the Pittsburgh Theological
Seminary, Pittsburg, PA, and the United Theological College, Bangalore

"In this comprehensive study on Telugu Christians, James Taneti, an 'insider,' commendably narrates the story of the appropriation of Christian faith by Dalits, Adivasis, and Caste communities. This work brings to the focus the role played by the women in Telugu Christianity, hitherto a neglected area. This study also critically examines the nonchurch and antichurch movements and those movements within the church that influenced the contextualization of Telugu Church."

—David Udayakumar Kurapati, professor of missiology and principal,
Master's College of Theology, Visakhapatnam, India

"Decolonising the Church involves decentering the denominational histories and writing the marginal communities into the history of the Spirit's movement. This book engages in such redemptive historiographic practice. A must-read for every student of Dalit Christian Studies."

—Joseph Prabhakar Dayam, professor of theology, Sam Higginbottom University
of Agriculture, Technology and Sciences, Allahabad, India

"James Taneti's focus on group conversions of the Telugu Dalits into Christianity in the late eighteenth and early nineteenth centuries and their part in the emergence of the local church, aspects hitherto neglected in the historical discourses, is commendable. This book is a resource to all those interested in studying and writing the history of Telugu Christians."

—Asheervadam Prabhudas Injumuri, professor of history of Christianity
and principal, Mennonite Brethren Bible Seminary, Shamshabad, India

# Telugu Christians

# Telugu Christians

## A HISTORY

James Elisha Taneti

Fortress Press
Minneapolis

TELUGU CHRISTIANS
A History

Cover design: Savanah N. Landerholm

Print ISBN: 978-1-5064-6943-0
eBook ISBN: 978-1-5064-6944-7

To my deceased grandparents—Taneti Veeranna, Buli Venkamma, Mandapalli Melenchthon, and Sugana— and all other ancestors, a part of whose story I am

# Contents

# Contents

# Acknowledgments

As any student of history would attest, it takes a village to work on a story. During the process of research and writing, I have consulted with and taken time from many colleagues in the Telugu states. These colleagues have been gracious with their time and wisdom. I have also sought data from archivists and acquaintances, and everyone approached has been generous. I am grateful for their patience and generosity. I am especially grateful to Arun Nirmal Raj, George Ebenezer, Larisa Peter, Rajendra Prasad Yarreballe, and Zaccheaus Katta for sending me books and documents when requested. Rosalyn F. Lomax has patiently looked at the style and accessibility of the draft, while John C. B. Webster generously commented on the argument and narrative. I am grateful to both. I, however, own responsibility for any flaws in style or substance. This delightful but laborious project would not have been possible without the untiring support of my wife, Mary, and children, Vismai, Vismitha, and Colt.

# Abbreviations

| | |
|---|---|
| AELC | Andhra Evangelical Lutheran Church |
| BFBS | British and Foreign Bible Society |
| BFMULCA | Board of Foreign Missions of the United Lutheran Church in America |
| CBFMB | Canadian Baptist Foreign Mission Board |
| CLS | Christian Literature Society |
| CMS | Church Missionary Society |
| COG | Church of God in India |
| CSI | Church of South India |
| GDM | Godavari Delta Mission |
| IPC | Indian Pentecostal Church of God |
| ISPCK | Indian Society for Promoting Christian Knowledge |
| LMS | London Missionary Society |
| MVS | Maranatha Visvasa Samajam |
| *NCCR* | *National Council of Churches Review* |
| NTC | New Testament Church |
| PIME | Pontifical Institute for Foreign Missions |
| SPCK | Society for Promoting Christian Knowledge |
| SPG | Society for the Propagation of the Gospel |
| WME | World Missionary Evangelism |

# Part I

# 1

# Introduction

Telugu Christianity is a site of collaboration, compliance, and conflict among social groups, with their religious quests and the political aspirations behind them. The confluence of social groups in the Telugu Church and their social interests determine the trajectory of its faith development. Amateur observers and non-Christian neighbors identify the community with Dalits and women, two groups at the margins of Telugu society. As a child, I witnessed the gatherings of these Christians being publicly shouted at and heard discreet whispers about their "untouchable" origins and "feminine" religion. Even the caste Christians tend to identify Christianity with Dalits and hence call themselves "converts" and not necessarily Christians. Although there may be a hint of contempt behind these claims, they are not without merit.

Telugu Christianity is a religion of the marginalized. In the hundred years between the mid-nineteenth and mid-twentieth centuries, Dalits embraced it and filled the church pews and pulpits. During this period, Christianity on the subcontinent had grown exponentially. The growth of Christianity was so phenomenal that Stephen Neill, a mission historian, claimed that Protestant Christianity on the subcontinent had grown tenfold in the second half of the nineteenth century.[1] It is difficult to account for the percentage of Dalits in the Telugu Church today,

---

1 Stephen Neill, *The History of Christian Missions* (London: Penguin, 1990), 309.

as many of them do not identify themselves as Christians due to
the implications it would have on their education and employment. The government of India designates a certain share of
seats in education and employment to Dalits, a provision aimed
at protecting the groups that have been wronged and ensuring
equity for all social groups. This affirmative discrimination is
also called "reservation." The Dalits who identify themselves
or are identified as Christians are denied this provision because
of a constitutionally agreed-upon claim that there is no caste
system in Christianity and that one cannot be a Christian
and Dalit at the same time.[2] Reservation is denied to Muslims and Parsees as well. Given the porous nature of religious
identities, Dalits and Christians may call themselves Hindus or
the census might record them as Hindus. Given the politics of
identity, it is both challenging and risky to accurately number
the percentage of Dalits within the church. Having consulted
with colleagues who specialize in the history of Telugu Christianity, I roughly estimate that at least three-fourths or more of
Telugu Christians are of Dalit background.[3] The lack of data
did not deter Solomon Raj Pulidindi, a Lutheran scholar, from
identifying the Telugu Christian community with Dalits.[4]

The women outnumbering the men in most Christian
gatherings signals the interest women show in Christianity. In

2  Prabhudas Asheervadam Injumuri, "The Dalits' Search for Identity in
   the Post-independent Era: A Study of the Dalit Christian Experience
   in the Prakasham District of Andhra Pradesh" (DTh diss., Senate of
   Serampore College, 2013), 4.

3  The church historians consulted include Prabhudas Asheervadam
   Injumuri, Srikanth Chittibabu Pavuluri, Ranjit Kumar Kanithi, Michael
   Kumar Chatterjee, and Chandra Sekhar Chakali. The suggested numbers were between vague "majority" and 90 percent. But all of them
   hinted at a number between 70 and 80 percent.

4  Solomon Raj Pulidindi, "Christian Prabhandha Literature," in *Striving for
   Excellence: Educational Ministry in the Church*, ed. Siga Arles and Brian Wintle
   (Bangalore, India: Center for Contemporary Christianity, 2007), 393.

addition to filling the pews, women—Dalit and "caste"—have been at the front lines of introducing the tradition to their families and communities and in inviting them to faith in Christ, as I will demonstrate in the following chapters. They continue to transmit and interpret the Christian tradition at home and in their communities.

Despite, or perhaps because of, their location at the social margins, Telugu Christians, by and large, are as Sanskritic as their non-Christian neighbors and occasionally more Hindu than others. The very values of which they found themselves victims and protested against to become Christian and the practices that perpetuated their subservience are the same values and practices an observer and non-Christian would find in them. For example, Telugu Christians do not lag behind their dominant caste counterparts in practicing endogamy, a system designed to cement caste boundaries and the control of women. This riddle prompted the rendering of this story. I seek to explain this conundrum of the marginalized mimicking the dominators by analyzing the social processes at work in the making of Telugu Christianity. The aim of this volume is two-pronged and modest. It is, first, to narrate the story of Telugu Christians and while doing so, second, to demonstrate how the social interests of social groups shaped the reception, interpretation, and appropriation of their religion.

While attempting to analyze the processes of reception, interpretation, and appropriation of Christianity by Telugus, I draw from the masterly work of Lamin Sanneh in his book *Translating the Message: The Missionary Impact on Culture*.[5] Examining various episodes of vernacularization in the history of Christianity, Sanneh points to how the translatability of the Christian message undermines possible attempts by the preacher to

---

5  Lamin Sanneh, *Translating the Message: The Missionary Impact on Culture* (Maryknoll, NY: Orbis, 1989).

elevate their culture and stigmatize the culture of the hearer. Every preaching of Christianity is an encounter of two cultures, that of the preacher and that of the hearer. The preacher transmits the message, and the hearer, out of their cultural worldview, appropriates it. Sanneh considers these processes of transmission and appropriation as basic to the translation of the Christian message. The principle of translation theologically inherent in Christianity invariably affirms the worldview enveloped in the local language.[6]

What if two groups speak the same language and yet subscribe to different worldviews and power interests? In the case of Telugu Christians, the appropriation of the Christian faith involved more than one worldview. It included the worldviews of Dalits, Adivasis, and the myriad "caste" communities. In becoming Christians, converting groups abandoned some of their beliefs and practices and retained others. At the same time, they reinterpreted and internalized parts of the Christian messages to fulfill their interests and aspirations. In these processes of abandoning parts of the old, retaining some, and appropriating elements from the new and together forging a new faith community, there were losses and gains, some volitional and others negotiated. Those with social leverage dominated this complex negotiation. The power equations between the preacher and the recipients as well as among the recipients invariably impacted the process of translation. In the process, though numerically dominant, Dalits and women had yielded more than their dominant caste counterparts had in the appropriation of the new faith. With social respect as their goal, Dalits and women, even while embracing Christianity, have subscribed to Sanskritic values and practices, what M. N. Srinivas, a sociologist, calls the process of Sanskritization. Srinivas defines this process as the one through which groups from the lower strata of

---

6 Sanneh, 1.

society emulate the customs, rituals, ideologies, and lifestyles of the dominating castes to climb the social ladder.[7] He lists religious conversions, neo-Vedantic movements, and Sanskritization as weapons of the "low" castes in their demands for better social status.[8] I argue that the processes of Christianization and Sanskritization have been parallel for Telugu Christians. I consider the practices of endogamy and the hierarchy based on caste and gender as the markers of Sanskritization.

The process of Christianization invariably involved incorporating a certain degree of modernity. Colonial and missionary collaboration in the late nineteenth and early twentieth centuries made literacy accessible to Dalits. Despite having to choose between livelihood and school, Dalit Christians, by and large, took advantage of the opportunities. Not all could afford to risk lives and livelihood. Having acquired some level of education, many have pursued occupations beyond agriculture, scavenging, and leather-processing, the ones required of Dalits by the traditional Telugu society. And in the process, they moved from receiving wages in kind to a cash-based economy. The move toward literacy, nontraditional employment, and a cash economy had a social agenda as well as implications on their social status. Thus the goal of social respect has been a common thread in the processes of modernization and Sanskritization. The Telugu Christians are by-products of these processes.

To demonstrate how the social interests and political milieu of the Telugu Christian communities impacted their negotiation with the worldview of the Western preachers and with their own, I have divided the book into two sections. While the first narrates the tale of Telugu Christians in the shadow of Western colonialism—Portuguese, Danish, French, Dutch, and

---

7  M. N. Srinivas, *Social Change in Modern India* (Bombay: Allied, 1966), 7.
8  Srinivas, 7.

British—the second section focuses on the developments in the postcolonial era. This division acknowledges the role political milieu plays in the evolution of a faith community.

The second chapter analyzes the sporadic and scattered interactions among Telugus in the sixteenth, seventeenth, and eighteenth centuries. The sites of these encounters and the social location of the converts point to the origins of Telugu Christianity, and the literature produced during the period exposes the dominance of the literati—local and European—in its evolution. The missionary focus had been on the dominant groups, and the favorable responses had been from the Sudhra castes. The Telugu Christian literature produced by both natives and European missionaries communicated the Christian faith in the idioms of the caste Hindus and thus subtly affirmed the worldviews of the dominators. Missionaries' mention of Dalits is rare in the period. This cryptic silence about or from Dalits can be interpreted as either a Dalit response in itself or missionaries' reluctance to engage Dalits in their efforts.

In the Telugu Church, three worlds converged, those of Western (Catholic and Protestant) missionaries, Dalits, and Hindus. The confluence—voluntary, negotiated, and necessary—of these worlds is the subject matter of the third chapter. Dalits converted as communities. They untapped the civil utility of the gospel. The dominant caste Christians, on the other hand, influenced the articulation of the Telugu Christian thought through the pen and pulpit. Western missionaries were not passive spectators in the process of translation. They validated the efforts of some groups more than others.

In the fourth chapter, I turn to the feminization of Telugu Christianity. The articulation of the faith occurred more in streets and homes than on pulpits. With their access to families and ears to the ground, women have mediated the Christian faith and modeled its piety. As Biblewomen, schoolteachers, and health professionals, they presented a Christ who cares for the immediate and holistic needs of individuals and families.

At the onset of political freedom in the mid-twentieth century, the British colonial administrators left, but not the Christian missionaries, at least not for the next three or four decades. There were movements both within the church and beyond that intentionally sought to integrate the local folk and classical traditions into the thought and practice of Telugu Christians. In the fifth chapter, I discuss the processes of devolution, of which the formation of the Church of South India (CSI) is an integral part, as well as the movements within these alignments. The popular religiosity in the CSI, new patterns of evangelism with the Andhra Evangelical Lutheran Church (AELC), and the continued influence of the bhakti tradition on the songs attest to the continued contextualization in the Telugu Church.[9]

The sixth chapter examines the nonchurch and antichurch movements. Critical of the ecclesiastical structures and Western liturgies, Devadas Mungamuri had established the Bible Mission and Bakht Singh Chabra the Hebron movement. Both movements were established in the 1930s but flourished only during the postcolonial era. Rejecting the notions of ecclesiastical offices and sacraments, Venkata Chalam Gudipati and Subba Rao Kalagara led Christ-centered movements among the Hindus. Chapter 7 summarizes how conflicting social interests

---

9 Bhakti is a tradition within Hinduism that stresses the faith in and devotion to a personal God (*swayam bhagawan* or *ishta daivam*). It is one of the three paths or disciplines with which an individual is believed to attain liberation, or *moksa*. The word *bhakti* literally means "sharing." A bhakta is believed to be sharing a relationship or bond with God. Arun Jones studied the confluence of bhakti tradition and American evangelicalism in another region in greater detail. See his book *Missionary Christianity and Local Religion: American Evangelicalism in North India, 1836–1870* (Waco, TX: Baylor University Press, 2017).

and the worldviews that emerged out of them coalesced in the Telugu Church.

The last three decades have ushered in a new era in the history of Telugu Christians. The government's decision under Prime Minister Vishwanath Pratap Singh to implement the recommendations of the Mandal Commission in 1990, the opening of the Indian market to foreign investors in 1991, and the demolition of the Babri Mosque in 1992 have significantly changed the political and cultural fabric of India as well as that of Telugus. Telugu Christians were no exception. Religious fundamentalism changed the texture of teachings and practices across the religions. The unregulated intrusion of foreign media and intense broadcasting of the prosperity gospel and commercialization of religion have affected Telugu Christianity. With at least two chief ministers (Sandinti Rajasekhara Reddy Yeduguri and his son, Sandinti Jaganmohan Reddy Yeduguri) from the community, Telugu Christians have also inched closer to political power and have become active in electoral politics even while professing to be otherworldly. This period has not been covered in this volume and hopefully will be studied in the future.

Before moving further, it would be appropriate to mention who these Telugus are. Telugus are a cluster of multiple social subgroups that share a common language. Declared so in 2008, Telugu is one of the six classical languages of India.[10] The classification as a classical language presumes the existence of a literary tradition for at least 1,500 to 2,000 years and a community that produced it. The oldest of the Telugu inscriptions dates back to the fourth century BCE. Telugus resided in or hailed from the regions that currently are the states of Andhra Pradesh and Telangana, as well as the Yanam district of Puducherry.

---

10  The other classical languages are Tamil, Sanskrit, Kannada, Malayalam, and Odia.

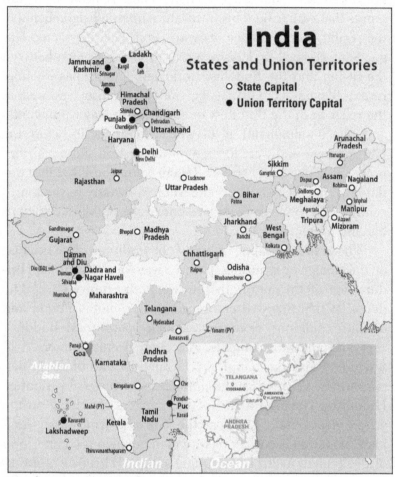

The Telugu states in modern India

Maximillian Dorbecker, "Administrative Map of India with States and Union Territories," Wikimedia Commons, January 18, 2020, https://commons.wikimedia.org/wiki/File:India_-_administrative_map.png.

There is no consensus about the origins of the community, nor does it serve our purposes here. There is, however, a consensus that earlier Buddhism was the earliest official religion in the region. The existence of words from Pali, the sacred language of classical Buddhism, attests to the association between the region and the Buddhist worldview. The stupas in Amaravati, Bhattiprolu, Ghantasala, and Jagayyapeta—as well as the relics from the Buddhist monasteries in Nagarjunakonda and Bheemunipatnam, all of which date back to before the Christian era and were located on the eastern shore—further prove the connection between Telugu culture and Buddhist tradition. Emperor Ashoka of the Maurya dynasty in the fourth century BCE not only embraced one of the Buddhist traditions but also promoted it abroad.[11]

The gradual disappearance of the tradition, often because of the change of dynasties, paved a way for the eventual Hinduization of the culture by the twentieth century CE.[12] The dynasties that followed embraced and promoted Hindu and Muslim traditions. Some occasionally patronized Buddhist sites and cultural elements. Although deeply immersed in Shaivism, with the temple in Tirupati as one of its principal shrines, Vaishnavism has influences in the local variant of Hinduism. Having warned of the dangers of relying on the government census, I will cite the data to provide an approximate, if not an accurate, picture of the religious composition of the Telugus in 2011. According to the 2011 census, approximately 90 percent of the 84.5 million Telugus residing in the region identified themselves or were identified as Hindus by

---

11  Those interested in the subject may see Sree Padma and A. W. Barber, eds., *Buddhism in the Krishna River Valley of Andhra* (Albany: State University of New York Press, 2008).

12  Trevor Leggert translated "Transmission of Buddhism to the Andhra Region" (*Middle Way: Journal of the Buddhist Society* 77, no. 4 [February–April 2003]: 224–25) from an anonymous Japanese source.

the census recorders. Accounting for less than 2 percent, more than one million of them identified themselves as Christians and living in more rural than urban areas, and there were more women than men.[13] Most of the people I spoke with put the number three times higher. More than 7 percent of the total population identified themselves as Muslims.[14] There is a significant Telugu diaspora abroad.[15] There are Telugu congregations in South Africa, Myanmar, the United Arab Emirates, and various cities in North America and Europe. Recognizing my limitations and the need for clear scope, I will be studying the Telugu Christians in the states of Telangana and Andhra Pradesh.

If there are Christians who identify themselves as Hindus either because of the loss of government or because they simply see Hinduism more as a culture than a religion, who are the Christians I am studying? Before responding to the question, one needs to be reminded that the question of religious identity is complex and fluid. As mentioned earlier, an individual may see themselves as a Christian while in church and as a Hindu at a social event, such as a wedding or a funeral in their neighborhood. When asked about their faith, non-Dalit Christians—even second- or third-generation Christians—at best would identify themselves as converts to be distinguished from Dalits, with whom Christianity is associated. Although there is a clause on religion, the question of religious identity is rarely posed to Christians. Given my experience, I would be surprised to hear a census taker ask an individual about their

---

13  The government census is from "C-1 Population by Religious Community," Office of the Registrar General and Census Commissioner, India, accessed December 16, 2020, https://www.censusindia.gov.in/2011census/C-01.html.

14  "C-1 Population."

15  There are more than four hundred thousand Telugus in the United States alone.

religious identity. For Dalit Christians, such a question sounds more like a legal threat than a routine query. Among the caste Christians, the identity as a Christian carries a stigma, and they seldom reveal their religious identity in public. Given the porous nature of the religious identities, I have considered those groups that profess faith in Christ and practice the rites of baptism and the Lord's Table.

As I have mentioned earlier, the majority of Telugu Christians are Dalits. I will be commenting later in the book when necessary, but it would be helpful here to describe briefly the caste system among the Telugus and the place of Dalits in it. Like most others on the Indian subcontinent, Telugu society is stratified into castes. An individual's birth determines their caste identity, occupation, social status, and geographical location. The classical four-tiered caste hierarchy—with Brahmins at the top, Sudhras at the social base, Kshatriyas and Vaishyas in between, and Dalits outside the system—does not apply in Telugu society. In this agrarian society, the landowning Sudhra communities control land, natural resources, human labor, and thus the power balance. Brahmins, Vaishyas, and Kshatriyas provide supportive religious, economic, and administrative systems. Brahmins see themselves as custodians and transmitters of traditions, deciding when and how to be catalysts of change. They, interpreting the religious texts, officiate rituals, teach "normative" language, and commit the present to future generations through texts, songs, and stories. Kshatriyas traditionally were the custodians of the territory, but their social influence has been curtailed by legislation during and after the colonial period. They are rare among the Telugus, and some of them use their inherited lands and legacies as means of social influence. Through their control over the market and industry and with their skills to negotiate with producers, Vaishyas are the power brokers. On a day-to-day basis, they engage in businesses—small and big. Denied a share in the land and to make ends meet, Dalits provide cheap labor to the landowning Sudhras.[16]

The cluster of communities considered outcastes by the dominators identify themselves as Dalits. Just as the term *Dalit* does not connote one singular community with shared practices and interests, the four categories in the *varna ashrama dharma* (a system based on caste or color) include numerous subcastes with shared and conflicting interests. In addition to Madigas and Malas, numerous other communities are listed as Scheduled Castes, the legal term to refer to Dalits.[17] There are hundreds of subcastes among the Sudhras and dozens among Brahmins, none equal to another. Thus there are not only myriad groups in every category, but each has a hierarchy. In this volume, my references to the terms *Dalits* or *Sudhras* are broad and include the subcastes within each category. When certain of the name of the subcaste or if naming the subcaste helps the argument, I have referred to it with its specific name, such as Mala and Madiga.

In addition to the inter- and intracaste rivalries, the control of women is another mechanism used to cement and perpetuate the caste system. Since individuals are born into a caste and inherit both the properties and the social status at birth, the beneficiaries of the caste system recognize women's potential to dismantle it and therefore created a culture that not only polices women's procreative activities but also regulates their relationships in personal and social spheres. The restrictions on women vary. The higher their caste in the hierarchy, the more stringent the restrictions on them are.

The concentration of power among some and the denial of social space to others are religiously sanctioned. The dominators and their allies justify and preserve the system by citing Hindu mythologies and scriptures, such as Manu Dharma.

---

16  Ilaiah Kancha and Padma Rao Katti reinterpret some of these traditions in their writings and interviews.

17  Fifty-seven more communities are listed as Scheduled Castes nationally.

They require Dalits to engage in occupations that could be considered defiling, such as scavenging. They considered Dalits to be ritually impure and therefore, in the past, to be physically defiling. The practice of untouchability was abolished in 1955 but not the system that caused the practice.[18] The landowning communities continue to extract Dalit labor, and the local administrations demand their services.

In their bid to curve space and possibly restructure the power symmetry, the victims of the caste system developed alternative worldviews. The divine is capable of suffering, and suffering is an indispensable divine attribute. Moreover, the divine is feminine. I will discuss in chapters 3 and 4 more of the Dalit cultures.

Titles tell stories. They inspire stories. And here is the story behind this book title. The inspiration for this modest project traces back to two titles: First, Antonius Kroot's *History of the Telugu Christians*.[19] Kroot, a Catholic friar of the St. Joseph's Missionary Society of Mill Hill, recounts the origins and expansions of the Catholic communities among the Telugus. To reconstruct this history, he had extensively consulted letters from European Catholic missionaries. Published in 1910, Kroot's book is a product of its times. Like most of its contemporaries, the scope of the book is limited to the confessional family that the writer represents. Kroot was inclusive to have included the work of other Catholic missionary orders in the region. Catholic missionaries and their missionary efforts among the Telugus are the focus of this monumental work, whereas in my work, Telugu Christians—a faith community, native but connected to the global church—are the subject matter.

The title of John C. B. Webster's *The Dalit Christians: A History* was another source of inspiration.[20] In this defining work,

---

18 India Const., art. XVII.

19 Antonius Kroot, *History of the Telugu Christians* (Trichinopoly, India: Mill Hill St. Joseph Society, 1910).

20 John C. B. Webster, *The Dalit Christians: A History* (Delhi: ISPCK, 1994).

Webster highlights the agency and agenda of the Dalit Christians and locates the religious choice of the Dalit communities in the context of the latter's movements for social dignity. He demonstrates how the social aspirations of a community shape its religious beliefs. In this volume, I acknowledge the impact of social interests and political dynamics on belief systems but at the same time highlight the conflicting interest groups within the Telugu Christian community. Although the majority of the church is Dalit, numerous caste communities and their social interests constitute the Telugu Church.

Given the subject matter, Christians in South Indian Villages, 1959–2009: Decline and Revival in Telangana by John B. Carman and Chikuri Vasantha Rao. Carman in collaboration with P.Y. Luke has earlier studied the folk practices of the rural Christians in Telangana. Marking the fiftieth anniversary of the study, he has teamed with eight seminarians from Andhra Christian Theological Seminaries led by Chilkuri Vasantha Rao identifies the influences of Pentecostal and Holiness spiritualities on the Church of South India Christians in the region. The study covers the period that I do not and its scope is limited to the Church of South India. It sheds light on the popular expressions of Christianity in rural Telangana.

Finding accurate statistics for Christian communities and data for history from churches has been a challenge. The churches with Dalit Christians ordinarily do not keep church records, lest they become evidence against their families in case of a government investigation. There were several instances of Dalits losing their Dalit status and thereby their constitutional rights because of their connection with a Christian community. Moreover, those "nondenominational" groups that view mutual accountability and record keeping as not congruent with the New Testament churches leave little data for a historian to work with. With an exception of Chinna Rao Yagati, Telugu historians ordinarily locate Christians either at the edges of or outside the

Dalit community.[21] Most historians tend to relegate Dalits to
the margins or even outside the scope of their research.

I have gratefully and carefully gleaned from the following data of primary sources: First, the voluminous missionary
records appeared to be and proved to be fertile sources, but they
were not as productive as I anticipated them to be.[22] Telugu
Christians are the subject of my study; missionaries' sacrifices
and accomplishments were reported in the missionary records.
After all, missionaries were reporting to their donors invested in
their work and were seeking further investment. Telugu Christians were occasionally mentioned, but only as beneficiaries of
missionary services. The identities and social locations of the
Telugu Christians were seldom identified but as vaguely as possible. If social locations of native Christians were identified, it
was mostly to celebrate Christians of dominant caste descent as
individual "trophies."[23]

Second, the books and songs written by Telugu Christians
proved to be invaluable sources. However, there is a considerable
caste imbalance in the sources, as most of these writers were of
dominant castes. Having hailed from oral traditions and acquired
literacy as their second mode of communication, Dalit Christians,
by and large, did not leave many literary records. In their absence,
I interpreted references about them by missionaries or colonial
chroniclers. I have extensively but carefully consulted Telugu
Christian commentators, such as Ratna Sundara Rao Rayi,

---

21  Chinna Rao Yagati, *Dalits' Struggle for Identity: Andhra and Hyderabad,
    1900–1950* (New Delhi: Kanishka, 2003).

22  I have discussed the challenges and opportunities of writing the history
    of Telugu Christians from these sources in an earlier work: James Elisha
    Taneti, *History of the Telugu Christians: An Annotated Bibliography* (Lanham,
    MD: Scarecrow Press, 2011), 1–16.

23  John Craig et al., eds., *Telugu Trophies: The Jubilee Story of Some of the Princi-
    pal Telugu Converts in the Canadian Baptist Foreign Mission in India from 1874 to
    1924* (Toronto: CBFMB, 1925).

Joe Sebastian, Solomon Thanugundla, Solomon Raj Pulidindi, and Evangeline Bharathi Nuthalapati.

Third, colonial record keepers and so-called Indologists, for their administrative purposes and colonizing agenda, produced capacious literature, parts of which I scanned carefully and that occasionally resonated with some of the oral stories folks tell and retell in rural India, a world in which I grew up, and thus can shed light on the ritual practices and traditional occupations of the Dalits. I am well aware of the colonizing agenda behind collecting these stories. Together, these sources provided me with the data critical to reconstructing the story of Telugu Christians.

Historians mediate between two worlds, the world of those whom they study and the world of those whom they are addressing. It is a blessing and a curse at the same time. Whenever I undertake a writing project, I remind myself that the present looks up to connect it with the past, and the past deserves to be represented with utmost care. Neither celebrating nor cursing either is my job. However, I consider respecting both worlds as an obligation.

A warning is due here. As a Telugu Christian, I am a part of this tale. Being an insider gives some advantages. An insider sees and hears things that an observer does not see and hear. There were numerous occasions in this story where I did not have to depend on a written source. As mentioned earlier, Telugu is an ancient language, with its script and literary tradition. But most of the Telugu Christians have come from communities with oral traditions. They have told and transmitted their stories. I have been a beneficiary of that rich tradition. Given my identity, I have also had the trust of the people I interviewed, something that colleagues from other linguistic groups have to earn. Telugus were gracious in sharing the information they have at hand and telling me stories they are aware of.

Here is an assurance. I remained aware of and alert to two possibilities: First, with trust comes expectation. Some of those who invested trust, time, and their stories might expect their interpretations to be parroted. Second, insider writers also have their attachments and commitments that may either clarify or blur the interpretation of the story. My multiple but fluid identities as a Dalit Telugu Christian man may have shaped my lens and rendering of the story. My commitment to and involvement in the art of history writing however have taught me to consider my community as deserving of careful and critical examination. As a student of history, I am accountable to my colleagues, current readers, and future researchers. When you read through the following pages, be alert that I am a part of the story, but be assured that as a sincere student of history with a commitment to the objective interpretation of the communities, I have made every effort to locate myself apart from it. Now let us turn our attention to the story of the Telugu Christians.

# 2

# Scattered Beginnings

It cannot be ascertained as to when Telugus came into contact with Christianity. The evidence available suggests that they heard of Christianity in the early modern period, if not before. Roman Catholic missionaries from Europe were the first ones to introduce Christianity to them. The five missionary orders that missionized in the region include Franciscans, Jesuits, Theatines, Augustinians, and Carmelites. As in other regions of the sub-continent, Catholic missionaries focused on Christianizing the natives, especially those of the dominant groups, hoping that the conversion of the rulers would ultimately draw the subjugated to Christianity. This pattern of reaching the social elite continued even into the nineteenth century. Missionaries' affinity with European colonial powers aided this strategy.

As a result of the evangelizing efforts of European Catholic friars, families and individuals of the landowning communities—namely, Kammas, Reddys, and Velamas—became Christian. Although these Christians cannot be located at the top of the traditional caste hierarchy, by virtue of their control of land and labor, they were both influential and dominant. Roman Catholic missionaries sought and found the patronage of the native rulers. By and large, Christianity was a religion of the elite in the first three centuries, and its texture invariably was Sanskritic. Meanwhile, Protestant missionaries located in Vepery reached Telugus in the eighteenth century. They taught literacy and translated the Bible into Telugu. This chapter provides a general account of the beginnings of Telugu Christianity in the early modern period, especially that of the interactions between Telugus and Christian missionaries from Europe.

## Traditions

Before narrating the documented contacts of Telugus with Christianity, it is pertinent to mention recent claims about earlier beginnings. Just as Thomas Christians claim that their church is as ancient as Christianity itself, some church historians date the presence of Christianity in coastal Andhra back to the first century. Thomas Christians in South India believe that Thomas, one of the disciples of Jesus, preached in the present states of Kerala and Tamil Nadu and gathered worshipping communities there.[1] Echoing the Thomas tradition, an anonymous essay, which was later deleted, attributes the beginnings of Christianity in Andhra to migrations from Alexandria in the first century.[2] The claim appears plausible, as Alexandria was one of the prominent centers of Christianity in the first century. Also, located on the coast, the city of Machilipatnam could have been an attractive destination for merchants and migrants from abroad, just as port cities in the southeastern and southwestern coasts were.

Silent about the Christian presence in the first three centuries, this tradition alludes to an existing Christian community in Machilipatnam in the fourth century. It does not, however, mention the community's faith or its practices. Its advocates buttress

---

1 Mathias Mundadan accounts for and evaluates the Thomas tradition in the volume *History of Christianity in India: From the Beginning up to the Middle of the Sixteenth Century* (Bangalore, India: Church History Association of India, 1989), 1:9–64.

2 "Ministry of the Catholic Church in Andhra Pradesh," Andhra Pradesh Bishops' Council, accessed November 30, 2020, http://www.apbc.in/images/News.pdf (URL is invalid).

their argument with a document from one of the ecumenical councils. One of the delegate-bishops is believed to have represented "dhivi." The advocates of this theory interpret this "dhivi" as Diviseema, an island adjacent to Machilipatnam. I hesitate to support this claim. There is no evidence strong enough to suggest that there was a native Christian community in the first century or the fourth century. Neither has the document cited its source or the author. Moreover, it cannot be concluded with certainty that the allegedly mentioned dhivi refers to Diviseema or any other coastal city in the region. *Dhivi* literally means "an island." There are competing claims of Christian presence in other islands in the Indian Ocean, such as Maldives. Even if dhivi referred to Diviseema, it was likely that the territory was under the ecclesiastical jurisdiction of a bishop and does not necessarily mean that there was an existing community. To the disappointment of those promoting this tradition, no community claims its origins from or continuity with a Christian community from these periods, nor are there sites or artifacts to support the tradition.

## Telugu Christians in the Sixteenth Century

The sixteenth century had been one of the most tumultuous and transforming periods in the history of Christianity worldwide. In addition to the reforms and renewal within and outside the Roman Catholic Church, the period had also marked the globalization of the Catholic tradition. It had witnessed the emergence of Protestant Christianity. We do not know much about Telugu Christianity in the sixteenth century except for a few initial encounters between the Telugus and Catholic missionaries from Europe. In his illuminating book, Joe Sebastian, an ecclesiastical historian, lists at least four such interactions.[3]

---

3 Joe S. Sebastian, *The Jesuit Carnatic Mission: The Foundation of the Andhra Church* (Secunderabad, India: Jesuit Province Society, 2004), 44.

As mentioned earlier, the focus of the Roman Catholic missionary efforts was mostly but not always on the social elite. We need to locate these efforts in the context of Jesuit missionary activities in other regions of the Indian subcontinent. Francis Xavier, one of the founding members of the Society of Jesus, traveled to the southeastern coast of Tamil Nadu in 1542 and served there until his death ten years later.[4] As an apostle to the East, he had also traveled to other regions in Asia. While on the Indian subcontinent, Xavier resided with and advocated for the vulnerable fisheries on the Parava (Pearl) coast. He advocated for the rights of Parava Christians in the context of repeated attacks from the local or foreign traders. In defense of the Parava Christians, Xavier collaborated with colonial authorities and native princes in the region. The Portuguese presence in Goa and their colonial enterprise on the subcontinent facilitated these missionary activities, and the political alliances these created provided an environment for missionary intervention in the lives of the local Christians.

At the northern tip of the subcontinent, a group of Jesuits arrived and resided in the palace of Akbar, a Mughal emperor. At the invitation of the emperor, Rudolf Aquaviva, Antonio de Montserrat, and Francisco Henriques reached Fatehpur Sikri in 1580, and in his audience, they engaged in religious discourses with teachers of other faiths.[5] There were at least two more teams that engaged in these interfaith dialogues. The "Agra" mission of the Jesuits did not last long. These missionaries subtly sought the conversion of the emperor, a dream that was never realized.[6] Meanwhile, at the dawn of the seventeenth century, Roberto de Nobili, an Italian Jesuit, resided among the

---

4  Sebastian, 44.

5  Pierre Du Jarric, *Akbar and the Jesuits: An Account of the Jesuit Missions to the Court of Akbar* (London: RoutledgeCurzon, 2005).

6  Arnulf Camps, *Studies in Asian Mission History: 1956–1998* (Leiden: Brill, 2000), 33–103.

Brahmins in Madurai and focused on their Christianization.[7] He presented himself as a guru and clothed Christianity in Brahminical idioms. He was in contact with Telugus and may have baptized a Telugu Brahmin, whom we will discuss later in this chapter. It was during this period that another Jesuit missionary, Matteo Ricci, employed similar strategies to evangelize the royal families and literati in China.[8]

These approaches of the Jesuit missionaries and other Catholic missionaries in the region emerged in part due to the existing belief that the Christianization of the rulers would ultimately result in the conversion of the subjects. This notion may have been because of the European model of the church-state relationships that in many ways culminated in the seventeenth-century Peace of Westphalia, signed in 1698. In this context of European colonialism on the subcontinent and with the notions born out of and imported from the church-state relationships in Europe, Luis da Salvador, a Franciscan friar, arrived in the Telugu province in 1510, more than three decades before the arrival of Francis Xavier.[9] According to the Padroado understanding, the monarchs in Europe appointed the missionaries, and the local colonial administrators funded them. Deputed by Pedro Álvares Cabral, Portuguese colonial administrator at Goa, and representing the Portuguese interests, da Salvador negotiated trade treaties with Vijayanagar rulers.[10] The Vijayanagar Empire ruled most of the southern part of the subcontinent. In addition to promoting the commercial and political interests of

7 Vincent Cronin, *A Pearl to India: The Life of Roberto de Nobili* (New York: E. P. Dutton, 1959), 85–87.

8 Jonathan D. Spence, *The Memory Palace of Matteo Ricci* (London: Penguin, 1985).

9 Sebastian, *Jesuit Carnatic Mission*, 44; Achilles Meersman, *The Friars Minor or Franciscans in India, 1291–1942* (Karachi, Pakistan: Rotti, 1943), 138.

10 Sebastian, 44. See also Solomon Thanugundla, *Structures of the Church in Andhra Pradesh: An Historico-Juridical Study* (Secunderabad, India: Karuna Sri, 1977), 14.

the monarch, da Salvador also introduced Christianity in the palace, two prominent aspects of sixteenth-century missionary activism. His service to his king and God ended abruptly when he was murdered in 1512.[11] The murder of an individual who was both a religious teacher and a political emissary surely was a local response, loud and clear, but we do not have sufficient data about the assassins, either of their motive or of their social location. John Carman, an expert on the folk religions of South India, holds a Brahmin guilty for this violent response, while Solomon Thanugundla blames a Muslim.[12] Even while complicating the nature of this response, it points to the alliance between the religious and political interests of the day. The Vijayanagar Empire was spread in most of South India, and its subjects included Kannadigas, Malayalees, Tamils, and Telugus.

Antonio de Padrao, another Franciscan missionary, followed his martyred colleague around 1530.[13] He moved beyond the palace. With royal permission, he preached his faith in the province. The response to de Padrao's teaching was less violent compared to the one da Salvador received. Families belonging to the weaver, herder, and toddy-tapping castes converted to Christianity.[14] The church among the Telugus thus had its beginnings among the marginal groups. De Padrao is believed to have built a church for them.[15]

### Telugu Christians in the Seventeenth Century

Jesuit missionaries arrived in the region at the dusk of the sixteenth century. Francis Ricci and Simon de Sa approached

---

11  John Carman and Vasantha Rao Chilkuri, *Christians in South India: 1958–2008* (Grand Rapids, MI: Eerdmans, 2014), 33.

12  John Leoncini, *A History of the Catholic Diocese of Vijayawada* (Secunderabad, India: Vani, 1988), 15.

13  Sebastian, *Jesuit Carnatic Mission*, 44.

14  Carman and Chilkuri, *Christians in South India*.

15  Sebastian, *Jesuit Carnatic Mission*, 44.

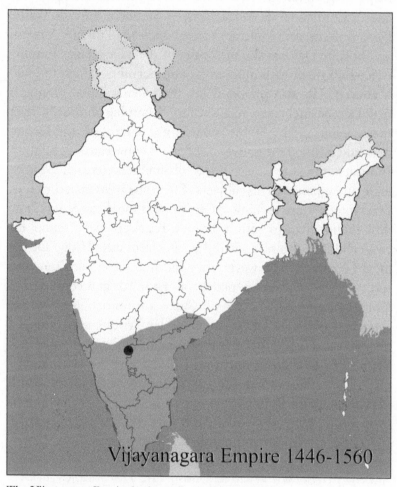

The Vijaynagara Empire in the early modern period

Mlpkr, "Vijaya Nagara Empire Map," Wikimedia Commons, January 17, 2007,
https://commons.wikimedia.org/wiki/File:Vijayanagara-empire-map.svg.

Vankatapathi Raju Devarayalu through his father-in-law, Obi
Raju, in 1598 and arrived at the palace in Chandragiri a year
later.[16] Emmanuel de Veiga, Gasper Stephen, John de Costa,
Peter Eutitius, and Melchior Cotinho followed them.[17] Vankatapathi Raju Devarayalu, then ruler of the Vijayanagar Empire,
welcomed them with open arms and permitted them to build
a church. He also provided for their living costs, forging a
benefactor-beneficiary relationship. Claiming authority over
the religious affairs of his subjects, the king went the second
mile and granted the natives freedom to convert to Christianity.
In return, the king expected the missionaries to teach Western
logic and sciences to his subjects. The friars resided in the court
for eighteen years, seeking to Christianize the dynasty and forge
diplomatic alliances with it. Francis Ricci opened a school for
caste children. He translated the catechism into Telugu for the
local Christians.[18] However, they did not accomplish much in
terms of conversions. Six people of "caste" origins converted to
Christianity in the first year.[19] There are no details on where
these converts were on the social ladder. Writing after almost a
decade, one of the missionaries, Antonio Rubino, lamented that
there were only fifteen converts in the mission.[20] The Chandragiri mission did not last after that either because of the death
of Vankatapathi Raju Devarayalu or because of the summons
from King Philip III of Spain and Portugal.[21]

---

16  Joseph Thekkedath, *History of Christianity in India: From the Middle of the
    Sixteenth to the End of the Seventeenth Century, 1542–1700* (Bangalore, India:
    Church History Association of India, 1982), 2:210.
    The missionaries belonging to the St. Joseph's Missionary Society
    were also called the Mill Hill Missionaries. St. Joseph's Missionary Soci-
    ety was founded in 1866.
17  Sebastian, *Jesuit Carnatic Mission*, 46.
18  Thanugundla, *Structures*, 22.
19  Sebastian, *Jesuit Carnatic Mission*, 46.
20  Thekkedath, *History of Christianity*, 2:211.
21  Thanugundla, *Structures*, 23. Cf. Thekkedath, *History of Christianity*, 2:211.

Both Henry Heras, an expert on the Vijayanagar Empire, and Antonius Kroot, a Mill Hill missionary, allude to the Christianizing agenda of the Jesuit mission in Chandragiri.[22] Much like the Jesuit mission at the Mughal court, there may have been diplomatic and trade motives in the Chandragiri mission. The local princes, seeking diplomatic and trade relationships with the Portuguese colonial powers, welcomed the Jesuit missionaries to their courts. Earlier, Rama Raju of the Tuluva dynasty made an economic pact with the Portuguese administration in the middle of the sixteenth century.[23] Vankatapathi Raju Devarayalu of the Aravidu dynasty would have continued his alliance with the Portuguese administration at Goa due to the continued threats from Ali Adil Shah I and Murtuza Khan. At the same time, one cannot altogether brush aside Jesuit missionaries as mere political surrogates or trading agents of Portugal. Like their contemporaries in Europe and other parts of Asia, they may have been committed to Christianizing the peoples on the Indian subcontinent. For them, loyalty to God and loyalty to the king went hand in hand.

If Christianizing was the lone part of their agenda, fifteen conversions in ten years were not noteworthy. Kroot identifies the Jesuit missionaries' reluctance to adapt to the native culture as the reason for the dismal numbers. Working almost a century earlier, Francis Xavier, their Jesuit senior, was involved in a community conversion. Given his willingness to adapt, Roberto de Nobili had a considerable number of converts, but the community did not last after his death. Jesuit missionaries in the Chandragiri court were ambivalent toward the locals. They chose to work with the social elite but refused to accommodate their customs. According to Solomon Thanugundla, a

---

22  Henry Heras, *The Aravidu Dynasty of Vijayanagara* (Madras, India: B. G. Paul, 1927).

23  Terala Satyanarayana Sharma, *Vijayanagara Charitram: 1336–1680* [A history of Vizianagaram: 1336–1680] (Nallagonda, India: Sankranthi, 2003), 147.

church historian, the friars at Chandragiri were afraid of being dragged into a rites controversy as their colleagues in Madurai had earlier been.[24] Around this time, Jesuits in China were also embattled in the Chinese Rites Controversy.[25] The reluctance of Chandragiri missionaries to adapt to the local vestments earned them the stigma of *parangi*, or a "dirty one," alienating Christianity from the Vijayanagar rulers and their subjects.

Meanwhile, de Nobili, another Jesuit who arrived in 1606 in Madurai, adapted the dress, diet, and lifestyle of the local elite to earn their respect. Even while reaching out to converts of all castes, he singularly focused on Brahmins. In Madurai, a temple city, Brahmins reigned at least culturally. He resided in a Brahmin neighborhood and lived according to their purity norms. In addition to Tamil and Sanskrit, de Nobili mastered the Telugu language, which was the dialect of the rulers, and he composed canticles and hymns in the language.[26] Sivadharma, a Telugu Brahmin, taught de Nobili both Sanskrit and Telugu in 1608.[27] By teaching Sanskrit to a European, Sivadharma may have risked his life.[28] Sivadharma converted to Christianity eighteen months after meeting de Nobili and was promptly ostracized by his community.[29] He remained a steadfast supporter of the mission and methods of de Nobili. When local Brahmins sought to persecute de Nobili, Sivadharma protected

---

24 Thanugundla, *Structures*.

25 Andrew Ross, *A Vision Betrayed: The Jesuits in Japan and China, 1542–1742* (Maryknoll, NY: Orbis, 1994).

26 Thekkedath, *History of Christianity*, 2:216; C. B. Firth, *An Introduction to Indian Church History* (Madras, India: CLS, 1961), 118.

27 Firth, *Indian Church History*, 113.

28 Cronin, *Pearl to India*, 85–87. Citing Max Müller, Stephen Neill claims that de Nobili may have been the first European to learn Tamil. Neill, *History of Christian Missions*, 184.

29 Cronin, *Pearl to India*, 139. Cf. Ines G. Zupanov, *Disputed Mission: Jesuit Experiments and Brahmanical Knowledge in Seventeenth-Century India* (New York: Oxford University Press, 1999), 87.

him.[30] Besides Sivadharma, there was no mention of any other Telugu converting to Christianity in response to de Nobili's preaching. It was likely that there were a few, as the temple city was ruled by Telugu aristocracy, and there may not have been a need to translate the catechism into Telugu unless there was some degree of interest from Telugus in the city. The few Tamil converts attracted to Christianity under his influence did not distinguish themselves as Christians either.[31]

In the middle of the seventeenth century, Theatines arrived in the region. With them, Catholicism extended eastward and northward. Francesco Manco arrived in Golconda in 1640 and then moved to Machilipatnam, on the east coast. He was reported to have found existing Christians in the city.[32] The Jesuits from the Madurai mission likely evangelized in the region.[33] Local Christians complained of not having received Mass for more than three decades. Manco traversed between Hyderabad, Machilipatnam, and Bheemunipatnam from 1641 and served the Catholics therein until he died in 1646.[34] Four more friars accompanied by two brothers of the Theatine order arrived in 1649 to serve these Catholic communities.[35]

Another missionary order showed missionary interest in the region. Augustinian priests followed their Theatine counterparts in 1646.[36] They built churches in Machilipatnam and Hyderabad in 1652.[37] Meanwhile, Gaetano Monaldini arrived in Bheemunipatnam, a Dutch colony, in 1665 and evangelized there for twelve years. His colleague Bergamore joined the

---

30  Cronin, *Pearl to India*, 101–3.

31  Firth, *Indian Church History*, 120.

32  Sebastian, *Jesuit Carnatic Mission*, 45. See also Thanugundla, *Structures*, 37.

33  Firth, *Indian Church History*, 119.

34  Thanugundla, *Structures*, 37.

35  Thanugundla, 37.

36  Thanugundla, 40.

37  Sebastian, *Jesuit Carnatic Mission*, 45; Thanugundla, *Structures*, 40; Leoncini, *History of the Catholic Diocese*, 9.

station in 1675 but moved to Narasapuram and worked there until 1693.[38] Bergamore evangelized also in Palakollu, Ponnapalli (currently in the Guntur district), Coringa (now in the East Godavari district), and Srikakulam and there gathered worshipping communities.

The presence of European Catholics serving the existing European—Portuguese, French, and Dutch—colonial administrations and their military cantonments may have necessitated and facilitated their visits to these places and occasionally resulted in the conversions of the natives to Christianity. Located closer to the Bay of Bengal, these places were within reach of the Theatine friars.

The interest showed by Abdulla Qutub Shahi, the king of Golconda, seemed to have offset the travel difficulties that friars would encounter. The interest of the king in mathematics attracted and allowed for the missionary work of Capuchin priests in 1645.[39] The possible offer by the sultanate to the Capuchin missionary Ephraim illustrates the opportunities made available to the missionaries. Impressed by Ephraim's intellectual acumen, the sultanate is said to have offered to host Ephraim, provide him an ox and two servants, and build a house and church at its expanses, although the offer was not accepted by the friar.[40]

Peter Paul of Palma, a Carmelite priest, arrived in 1696. Carmelite missionary presence was not as sustained as that of others. Though declining toward the end of the century, the Jesuits had dominated the missionary work in the region. They, by and large, concentrated on Christianizing the dominant castes. Known for their legacy in higher learning and teaching, they

---

38  Thanugundla, *Structures*, 39.

39  Leoncini, *History of the Catholic Diocese*, 10.

40  Glen J. Ames, "Acts of Faith and State: The Goa Inquisition and the French Challenge to the *Estado da India c. 1650–1675*," *Portuguese Studies Review* 17, no. 1 (Summer 2009): 19–21.

presented themselves as gurus. With their journals and letters, they educated their compatriots about the land they chose to live in.

The reports about missionary wanderings, officiating masses, and starting schools do not point to anything more than the presence of Christians—either European or Telugu or both—in these coastal towns as well as in Hyderabad by the end of the seventeenth century. They do reveal the nexus among the visiting missionaries, colonial powers, and local princes and how this alliance facilitated the spread of Christianity among the Telugus.

## Telugu Christians in the Eighteenth Century

Carmelites arrived toward the end of the seventeenth century, and other orders continued their missionary work. Protestant missionaries joined the bandwagon. The focus continued to be on the upper strata of society. Many more communities embraced Christianity. It is appropriate to discuss briefly what else was happening in the region before we analyze the encounters between Telugus and the European version of Christianity.

Nizam-ul-Mulk Asaf Jah, a Mughal viceroy in the Deccan (literally, "the south"), captured the city of Hyderabad, marking the birth of the state of Hyderabad in 1724. His dominion extended to the coastal cities, such as Machilipatnam.[41] With the weakening of the Mughal dynasty in the north, the Nizams could consolidate their position in the Deccan as independent rulers of the province. They made alliances, controlled the revenue, engaged in wars, and made treaties at their will and according to their power interests. As in the case of any dynasty, they did not retain every territory they occupied but

41 Sripad Ram Sharma, *The Religious Policy of the Mughal Emperors* (Bombay: Asia Publishing House, 1972), 567.

consistently held on to a major territory in the Deccan until it was annexed by the Indian Union in 1948. During its reign, the dynasty had power claims from within the family and foes from the neighboring kingdoms, realities that opened the space for European military powers, especially those from France and Britain, to intervene in the administration of the state of Hyderabad. The favors provided or denied to the European missionaries and their Telugu allies organically depended on the power pendulum of the Nizams.

Meanwhile, the political map of the coastal districts had significantly altered. Colonel Francis Forde, who was active in the Battle of Plassey under the leadership of General Robert Clive, arrived in Visakhapatnam in 1756 and seized Machilipatnam from the French occupation three years later.[42] This was one of the battles in the Seven Years' War (1756–63) between Britain and France fought on foreign soil, while others took place on the American side. Unsettled by the British aggression and the subsequent defeat of the French, Salabat Jung, the fourth nizam of Hyderabad, ceded the coastal districts north of Guntur in 1766 to the British. The Circar of Guntur had been granted twenty-two years later, forming what was later known as the Northern Circars. This strip on the seaside, rich in fertile land and water resources, had become a part of the Madras Presidency under British colonial control.

The last saga—but a prominent one, staged mostly in Europe—was the suppression of the Society of Jesus in 1773. After a protracted tussle between the Jesuits and Portuguese monarchs, the pope had outlawed the society, a decision that choked the support system for its missionary activities abroad in terms of both resources and personnel. This, as a result, slowed down the evangelistic activities of the Catholics in general and Jesuits in particular—at least until the mid-nineteenth century.

---

42 Thanugundla, *Structures*, 7.

Having discussed the political climate of the eighteenth century, I will now narrate the story of Telugu Christians during the period.

Peter Mauduit, a French Jesuit, reached Punganur in 1701.[43] Emulating the local literati, he wore the saffron robes of a *sanyasi*, or Hindu monk. He invariably evoked favorable interest among the dominant castes, according to Kroot.[44] He was fluent in Tamil and Telugu.[45] Punganur was a home for both Telugus and Tamils. The first decade of the century witnessed eighty baptisms.[46] The earliest and the most significant of them involved a Velama woman's four sons. Mauduit baptized three sons and employed the oldest as a catechist.[47] This unnamed son is the first catechist in the region. The baptism of a Velama family and the elevation of a convert to the rank of a catechist give us a hint about the social location of the people Mauduit was hoping to Christianize.[48] Joe Sebastian identifies the social location of other converts as Reddy and Kamma, the landowning communities in the region.[49]

Even while baptizing three Velama siblings, Mauduit refused to baptize their mother along with them, a gesture reflective of his accommodation of the local norms regarding women. Men of dominant castes were often appointed as catechists according to the local gender norms.[50] Women, despite their activism, had been relegated to the margins. Ironically, da Salvador received

43 Kroot, *Telugu Christians*, 38.
44 Kroot, 38.
45 Edward Rene Hambye, *History of Christianity in India: Eighteenth Century* (Bangalore, India: Church History Association of India, 1997), 3:313.
46 Thanugundla, *Structures*, 61.
47 Kroot, *Telugu Christians*, 21.
48 Kroot, 21.
49 Sebastian, *Jesuit Carnatic Mission*, 74. Cf. Hambye, *Christianity in India*, 3:320.
50 Sebastian, *Jesuit Carnatic Mission*, 22.

the patronage of the *rajmata* (mother of the local king) in his preaching activity.[51]

Mauduit's colleague Philip de la Fontaine continued the tradition of accommodating the customs of the social elite after the former's death in 1711. Active in Chandragiri and Perukuru, adjacent to Chittoor, between 1709 and 1718, he presented himself as a Romapuri *sanyasi* (an ascetic from Rome) and followed the Brahminical lifestyle, with its purity norms.[52] This representation of Christianity drew dominant caste communities in Chandragiri and Perukuru to Christianity. It earned him the title of "Apostle of the Brahmins."[53]

While the focus was on the dominant castes, the toddy-tapping and weaver communities in Krishnapuram of the Anantapuram district converted to Christianity.[54] As anticipated, several Reddys of Maddigubba also became Christians in 1712.[55] The chief of the community, Anumanda Reddy, was appointed a catechist in Dharmaram, an adjacent village west of Maddigubba.[56] After the miraculous healing of their leader, Kapus from Maddigubba approached Etienne Le Gac in Krishnapuram and were baptized seven years later.[57] Kroot reports that by 1736, there were thousands of Christians in the Chittoor and the Anantapur districts.[58]

An increase in conversions precipitated resistance from the neighboring communities. Religious conversions unsettle the political asymmetry. Aware of the threat posed to their social status, local priestly classes Dasaris and Brahmins frequently

---

51  Sebastian, 74.

52  Thanugundla, *Structures*, 61.

53  *Gazetteer of the Nellore District Brought Up to 1938* (Madras, India: Superintendent Government Press; Delhi: Asian Educational Services, 2004), 81; Thanugundla, *Structures*, 61.

54  *Gazetteer*, 81.

55  Sebastian, *Jesuit Carnatic Mission*, 86.

56  Thanugundla, *Structures*, 66.

57  Hambye, *History of Christianity*, 3:316.

58  Kroot, *Telugu Christians*, 24.

resorted to violence against the converts.[59] Seeking relief from the rioters, Telugu Christians sought and found protection from the local kings. In his volume on the history of Christianity, Edward Rene Hambye, a church historian, lists several instances of persecution.[60] He does not, however, identify the reasons behind the group conversions and the power interests of the persecuting priests and protecting rulers.

There was an increased burst of missionary activity in the middle of the century. Other missionary orders continued the work but with decreased intensity. By 1745, an Augustinian friar was reported to have been serving the parishes in Narasapuram, Korangi, Bheemunipatnam, Visakhapatnam, and Golconda.[61] Gaetano Astiano, a Theatine priest, arrived in Hyderabad in 1759.[62] Two other Theatines, Joseph Maria Albuquerque and Custodius Joseph Aravio, joined him later. The caste converts from Rayalaseema scattered to the Nellore and the Guntur districts because of frequent famines and incessant persecutions. Catholics found shelter in French domains, such as Phirangipuram, Oleru, and Tummurukota, thus introducing Christianity to new neighbors and extending its geographical reach.[63]

The eighteenth century had also witnessed the flourishing of Christian literature in Telugu as well as the Telugu literature by Christians. Given the confessional nature of Christianity and parallels in their Hindu tradition, Telugu Christians revered books and articulated their faith in Telugu. Missionaries used writing to codify and communicate their religion. For example, Jean Calmette composed a Telugu-Sanskrit dictionary of

59 Thanugundla, *Structures*, 63–64.

60 Hambye, *Christianity in India*, 3:319–20.

61 Thanugundla, *Structures*, 44.

62 Thanugundla, 45.

63 Clarence H. Swavely, ed., *One Hundred Years in the Andhra Country: A History of the India Mission of the United Lutheran Church in America* (Madras, India: Diocesan, 1942), 172.

theological terms and produced a compendium of the Christian faith in Telugu entitled *Satya Veda Sara Sangraham* in the 1730s.[64] Collaborating with local Brahmins, Peter de le Lane, another Jesuit, compiled a volume on Telugu grammar and his colleague Peter du Pons on Sanskrit grammar—monumental works highly regarded by Sanskrit scholars even today. Inspired by Calmette, Mangalagiri Anandam, a Telugu Christian of Niyogi Brahmin background, composed the *Vedanta Rasayanam*, one of the four respected Catholic *Prabhandhas*, which we will discuss shortly.[65]

There was a gradual decline of Catholic missionary activism in the second half of the eighteenth century. The series of Carnatic Wars between French and British armies in the second half of the century; the occupation of Machilipatnam and Pondicherry by the British in 1759 and 1761, respectively; the accession of the Circars by the nizam in 1766; and the suppression of the Society of Jesus in 1773 contributed to this decline.[66] The Telugu Christian communities survived in the region under newly established vicariates.

Meanwhile, Protestant missionaries started reaching out to the Telugus. Located in Vepery, now in Chennai, Benjamin Schultze (1689–1760), one of the German Pietists and part of the Royal Danish mission, undertook the translation of the Bible into Telugu. While his predecessors Bartholomäus Ziegenbalg and Heinrich Plütschau focused on Tamils in and around Tharangambadi, Schultze set himself to work among the Telugus.[67] He had learned the Telugu language and started schools. In addition to a Telugu grammar in German, Schultze wrote

---

64 A copy of the compendium may be found at the British Library in London. Hambye, *Christianity in India*, 3:337.
65 Hambye, 3:338.
66 Sebastian, *Jesuit Carnatic Mission*, 141.
67 Peter Vethanayagamony, *It Began in Madras: The Eighteenth-Century Lutheran-Anglican Ecumenical Ventures in Mission and Benjamin Schultze* (Delhi: ISPCK, 2010).

at least six books in Telugu on theological themes. Prominent among his contributions was the Telugu translation of the Bible in 1734.[68] Telugu linguists question the adequacy of the translation and the dialect used therein.[69] Peter Schmitthenner explains that Schultze may have used the dialect of the Brahmins based in Chennai.[70] Having been printed in Germany, this translation might not have been for the Telugus. However inadequate or objectionable, Schultze may have had a Telugu Brahmin teaching him the language, and we are not sure if that teacher was a Christian. The Protestant missionary-linguists were long remembered not only for documenting the cultures on the subcontinent but also for introducing print culture in the region, a mark of modernity Protestant missionaries were instrumental in introducing.[71]

During the second half of the eighteenth century, Telugus produced theological literature. They include *Thobya Charithra* by Pingali Yellanna, *Vedanta Rasayanam* by Mangalagiri Anandam, *Anithya-nithya Vythyasam* by an unknown writer, and *Gnana Chinthamani* by Mallela Thimma Raju.[72] The production of *Prabhandhas*, which Solomon Raj Pulidindi studied, was prominent among them.[73] Addressing Nidamamilla Das, likely a Christian landlord associated with the French East India Company, Mangalagiri Anandam, a Brahmin Christian, composed the fictional conversation in *Vedanta Rasayanam* between a local Brahmin and a European missionary. Using the genre

---

68  John Stirling Morley Hooper and W. J. Culshaw, *Bible Translations in India, Pakistan and Ceylon* (Bombay: Oxford University Press, 1963), 87.

69  Peter Schmitthenner, *Telugu Resurgence: C. P. Brown and Cultural Consolidation in Nineteenth-Century South India* (New Delhi: Manohar, 2001), 233.

70  Schmitthenner, 233.

71  J. Mangamma, *Book Printing in India: With Special Reference to the Contribution of European Scholars to Telugu* (Kuppam, India: Dravidian University, 2010), 34.

72  Pulidindi, "Christian Prabhandha Literature," 394.

73  Pulidindi, 394. Pulidindi defined *Prabandhas* as poetry with an opening prayer (*praveshika*) and occasional references to the writer's ancestors.

of religious dialogue, Anandam summarizes the Christian tradition as represented by the Roman Catholic missionaries he came in contact with. This religious discourse primarily contains another conversation—"a story within the story," as Solomon Raj called it—between a Christian missionary and a local scholar located in Chikkaballapur, culminating in the conversion of the scholar.[74]

The climax of the story provides us with the redactional agenda of Anandam, which is to persuade the reader to embrace the Christian faith. Given the genre, it is also probable that this textbook had a catechetical value, instructing children and new converts about the faith they were born into or had converted to. In addition to offering us an insight into how the natives articulated their faith in Christ, *Vedanta Rasayanam* also hints at the social location of the eighteenth-century converts.

Consisting of 904 stanzas, each stanza with four lines, *Rasayanam* is divided into four cantos. The first canto expounds on the attributes of God, while the second narrates the beginnings of human history and the Gospel stories of Jesus's birth. The third section focuses on the public ministry of Jesus, while the concluding part of the treatise interprets the death and resurrection of Jesus Christ and explains Roman Catholic beliefs, especially about the sacraments.[75]

Acknowledging the possible accusation that *Rasayanam* holds the Christian faith in "Brahminical captivity," Solomon Raj defends the attempt as strategic to communicate with the upper strata of Telugu society.[76] He identifies the several imprints of Hindu traditions in this appropriation of the Christian tradition. Here are some examples. First, in the language used to address his benevolent patron, Anandam reinforces the local feudal system, in which some individuals deserve more

---

74 Arles and Wintle, *Striving for Excellence*, 399.
75 Arles and Wintle, 398–99.
76 Arles and Wintle, 409.

respect than others and those without power are born to serve those with power.[77] Second, two miracle stories from the Gospels find a place in this treatise. The stories of the recovery of sight to Bartimaeus and the return of Lazarus from death could be interpreted as Christianity's answer to the first two parts of the Upanishadic prayer, in which the worshipper asks the deity to lead her from ignorance (blindness) to knowledge and from death to life.[78] Third, there is a mention of the eight aspects (*astanga*) of yoga, the sixteen parts of *puja* (worship or offering), and the four *purusartha* (pathways to success).[79]

We have so far studied the Christian missionaries' propensity to find potential converts among the dominant caste communities and how the conversion of the latter impacted the appropriation of Christianity in the first three centuries. In the following chapter, we will analyze whether the trajectory of the translation of the Christian message had changed. How far has it become the faith of the people? In whose idioms has this new worldview been communicated, transmitted, and appropriated? What place did the majority of the converts have in the appropriation of the Christian message?

---

77  Arles and Wintle, 404.
78  Arles and Wintle, 403.
79  Arles and Wintle, 406.

# 3

# A Confluence of
# Three Worlds

Telugu Christianity in the nineteenth century emerged out of a
convergence of three worldviews. Dalit communities embraced
Christianity in groups. As a result, Christianity, a religion that
had thus far been confined to the landowning communities,
eventually became the religion of the Dalits.[1] As Christian
communities everywhere do, Telugu Christians in their conversion to Christianity retained some of their pre-Christian worldviews, both Hindu and Dalit. They also drew resources from
the evangelicalism of the Protestant missionaries.

Relegated to the social fringes, Dalits in the nineteenth
century either converted to religions such as Islam, Buddhism,
or Christianity or emulated the norms and practices of the
dominating caste communities. Sanskritization is a process
through which groups at the bottom of the social hierarchy
seek to improve their status by emulating those at the top.[2]
For example, Gudalas, classified as Scheduled Castes, retained

---

1 The term *Dalit* literally means "crushed" or "broken." Dalits are Indigenous ethnic groups outside the four-tiered Hindu society ranked least in
the social hierarchy. Relegated to the social and geographical edges of a
village, Dalits are considered ritually impure and are expected to perform
menial and manual roles.

2 M. N. Srinivas, *Religion and Society among the Coorgs of South India* (Oxford:
Clarendon, 1952), 30–31.

their occupation as shoemakers, and given the stigma of impurity attached to the leather, they stitched shoes from synthetic
material. They intentionally chose to live in caste neighborhoods, even if it involved temporary humiliation. By emulating the purity norms of their neighbors, Gudalas sought social
respect. Given the desire for social respect from both missionaries and caste Hindus, Telugu Christians simultaneously appropriated evangelicalism and bhakti traditions in their beliefs and
piety. With better access to missionaries and literacy, Brahmin
and other dominant caste converts dominated this evolution of
Telugu Christianity.

## Beginnings of Telugu Protestantism

At least four events shaped the evolution of Telugu Christianity: two in the North Atlantic world, another in South India,
and one across the continents. First, the twin birth of evangelicalism and the modern missionary consciousness in the late
eighteenth century brought European and American Christians to the subcontinent. At least fifteen Protestant societies
started their missionary activities among the Telugus in the
nineteenth century.[3] At least four Catholic missionary orders
arrived in the Telugu states in the same century.[4] With them

---

3  These were the following: LMS (1805), SPG (1826), Plymouth Brethren
   (1833), American Baptists (1935), Free Church of Scotland (1837), CMS
   (1841), American Lutherans (1842), American Reformed (1853), American Episcopal Methodists (1857), German Lutherans (1865), Canadian
   Baptists (1868), British Wesleyans (1878), Russian Mennonites (1889),
   Salvation Army (1895), and American Mennonites (1899). In addition,
   there were a few unaffiliated missionaries who either worked alone or
   collaborated with others.

4  The Missionaries of St. Francis de Sales came to Visakhapatnam in 1845.
   The PIME from Italy arrived ten years later. The Mill Hill Missionaries
   arrived later in 1875. Pallottines arrived in Secunderabad toward the end
   of the century.

arrived the emphasis on the Bible, Western education, and print media. The second wave of North American evangelical revivals in the 1830s bolstered Protestant missionary activity.

Second, the gradual consolidation of the British colonial powers and the transfer of power from the British East India Company to the queen in 1858 significantly influenced the spread of Christianity on the subcontinent. Even though the official policies of the East India Company and the queen did not favor cultural intervention, the local colonial officers of evangelical leanings subtly supported the Christianizing and "civilizing" agendas of the missionaries.

Third, on the Indian subcontinent, marginalized groups were organizing themselves to seek better social status in the second half of the nineteenth century. For example, Shanar women in South Travancore, an adjacent region, fought for legislation that would allow them to wear clothing over their breasts, just as their counterparts in higher castes did.[5] Meanwhile, Dalits in Ludhiana, another end of the subcontinent, embraced Christianity en masse, numerically swelling the church twofold between 1834 and 1857.[6]

Fourth, the cultural climate engineered by the marginalized on both continents shaped the motives of both missionaries and Telugu converts. Struggles for the emancipation of the slaves in North America resulted in the American Civil War and the subsequent declaration of abolition. Having witnessed those events in the United States in the 1860s, John Clough and Emma Rauschenbusch-Clough were prepared for similar struggles on the Indian subcontinent. Their openness to allying with the marginalized groups brought them closer to Dalits.

---

5 Joy Gnanadason, *A Forgotten History: The Story of the Missionary Movement and the Liberation of People in South Travancore* (Columbia, MO: South Asia Books, 1996).

6 John C. B. Webster, "Punjabi Christians," *Journal of Punjab Studies* 16, no. 1 (Spring 2009): 40.

## Brahmin Christians Dominate

As they did in the previous centuries, Western missionaries continued to seek conversions among the dominant castes and offered
avenues for the caste converts to shape Telugu Christianity. For
instance, sent by the Church Missionary Society (CMS), Robert T. Noble, a Cambridge alumnus, and Henry W. Fox, an
Oxford alumnus, arrived in Machilipatnam in 1840. Hailing
from an upper stratum in their home country, they focused their
energies on their counterparts in India. Noble started a school
to "impart liberal education to the young men of the upper
caste."[7] The notion that the conversion of the "upper" strata
of the society would eventually result in the conversion of even
those at the margins may have been another reason for this
move. As a result, most early catechists were of dominant caste
descent. Ordained in 1864, Bushanam Ainala, a Velama, and
Ratnam Manchala,[8] a Niyogi Brahmin, were the first native
deacons in the CMS.[9] Both were ordained priests two years
later. Through his translation of the Book of Common Prayer
and leadership at the seminary, Ratnam had been influential in
interpreting the Christian tradition in the local church.[10]

The pattern of appointing the men of dominant castes as
preachers continued until the late nineteenth century. For example, Canadian Baptist missionaries appointed Josiah Burder, a
Niyogi Brahmin from Srikakulam, as the first native pastor in
the Baptist church in Kakinada in 1874.[11] The appointment of a

---

7  "The Rev. Ainala Bushanam," *Church Missionary Gleaner*, March 1886, 27.

8  For more about Ratnam Manchala, see Rajaiah D. Paul, *Chosen Vessels:
   Lives of Ten Indian Christian Pastors of the Eighteenth and Nineteenth Centuries*
   (Madras, India: CLS, 1961), 116–34.

9  "Rev. Ainala Bushanam," 27.

10  Parumootil Joseph Thomas, *100 Indian Witnesses to Jesus Christ* (Bombay,
    India: Bombay Tract and Book Society, 1974), 18.

11  John Craig, *Forty Years among the Telugus: A History of the Mission of the
    Baptists of Ontario and Quebec, Canada, to the Telugus, South India, 1867–1907*

Brahmin preacher in a Dalit community when its Dalit founder, Marayya Taleru, was still alive attests to the caste biases of the missionaries. This preference for the men of caste origins was present in the state of Hyderabad as well. British Methodists found George Harding Kadari, a Naidu from Vizianagaram, as eligible and appointed him as the probationer for the ministry in 1884 in Medak.[12]

The Brahminical domination over the processes of transmission and appropriation started even before the appointments of native catechists and priests. It began when Catholic and Protestant missionaries employed Brahmins as their language teachers. Considering Brahmins as pundits in the Telugu language, Western missionaries relied on their linguistic skills to learn the Telugu language. As mentioned earlier, Sivadharma, a Brahmin, taught Telugu and Sanskrit to Roberto de Nobili in the seventeenth century. The language teacher for George Cran and Augustus Granges was a Brahmin.[13] Almost every report of language learning mentions a Brahmin teacher and the practice of learning the Telugu language (and culture) as long as the Western missionaries arrived on the subcontinent, despite the literacy acquired by the Dalits in the twentieth century. The Brahminical language used in the theological treatises and biblical commentaries produced by Western missionaries attests to the level of Sanskritic influence on the understanding of Telugu cultures.[14]

(Toronto: CBFMB, 1908), 318.

12  F. Colyer Sackett, *Vision and Venture: A Record of Fifty Years in Hyderabad, 1879–1929* (London: Cargate, 1931), 251.

13  John Hay, "London Missionary Society, Vizagapatam," in *Missionary Conference: South India and Ceylon, 1879* (Madras, India: Addison, 1880), 2:286.

14  Americus V. Timpany, *Compendium of Theology* (Cocanada, India: n.p., 1879); John McLaurin, *Telugu Commentary on the New Testament: Acts of Apostles*, vol. 4 (Madras, India: SPCK, 1902); John McLaurin, *Telugu Commentary on the New Testament: Gospel according to St. John*, vol. 3 (Madras, India: SPCK, 1906); John McLaurin, *Telugu Commentary on the New Testament: The First Corinthians to Philippians*, vol. 4 (Madras, India: SPCK, 1906).

With their emphasis on the Bible, Protestant missionaries started translating it right after they arrived in the region. As mentioned earlier, Benjamin Schultze undertook the translation of the Bible into Telugu and is reported to have completed it by 1734.[15] The Telugu used in the translation reflects that of Telugu Brahmins in Chennai.[16] Later in the century, Brahmin pundits in Serampore translated the Bible into Telugu, in a project undertaken by William Carey of the General Baptist Missionary Society. They completed translating and printing the New Testament by 1818. Meanwhile, with the help of Anandarayar, a Brahmin from Kadapa, the London Missionary Society (LMS) located in Visakhapatnam translated and printed the New Testament in 1818.[17] Thus, even while revitalizing the Telugu language, the process of Bible translation ensured the continuity of the Brahminical worldview among the Telugu Christians.[18]

The hymnal is another significant vehicle for the Brahminical domination of Telugu Christian thought and piety. In the absence of written confessions, Telugus articulate and communicate in hymns. Hymns also function as catechetical tools. Despite their meager numbers in the pews, the songs written by Brahmin bards are sung and their worldview internalized by Telugu Christians. Purushotham Chowdhari (1803–90), a Gouda Brahmin, had been a prominent voice in the formative years of Telugu Protestant Christianity. Ordained a catechist in 1836 by

---

15  Hooper and Culshaw, *Bible Translations*, 87. A copy of the manuscript is still on display at the Frankische Foundation in Halle, Germany.

16  Schmitthenner, *Telugu Resurgence*, 232.

17  Hooper and Culshaw, *Bible Translations*, 98; Rajaiah D. Paul, *Triumphs of His Grace: Lives of Eight Indian Christian Laymen of the Early Days of Protestant Christianity in India, Every One of Whom Was a Triumph of His Grace* (Madras, India: CLS, 1967), 134.

18  Y. Vittal Rao, *Education and Learning in Andhra under the East India Company* (Secunderabad, India: privately published by N. Vidyaranya Swamy, 1979), 177.

the LMS, Chowdhari served the mission for twenty-seven years and the Odisha Baptists for twenty-five years.[19] With more than 130 hymns, Chowdhari inculcated the bhakti ethos of a devotee's submission to a personal god. In place of Krishna or Rama, Christ becomes the object of personal devotion. Chowdhari's hymns invite the worshipper to recite the name of Jesus, imagine the passion of Jesus, and worship Jesus's feet.[20] Praise for the redeemer God, admission of guilt, and gratitude for the grace received are common threads in his hymns.[21] At least 70 of his hymns are listed among the nine hundred songs in the current *Andhra Chraistava Keertanalu*.[22] Protestants use this hymnbook during both their public worship and personal devotions, allowing themselves to be shaped by the piety of the authors. With 29 hymns still in use, Jagannadham Pulipaka (1826–96) is another Brahmin bard with a significant influence on Telugu Christian thought.[23] In summary, more than 10 percent of the songs listed in the hymnal were written by two Brahmin Christians alone. Including the hymns by other Brahmin writers and the songs' use throughout the subcontinent would further

---

19 John Chowdhari, *Biography of the Rev. Purushottam Chowdhari* (Madras, India: CLS, 1906), 27.

20 Ravela Joseph, *Bhakti Theology of Purushottam Choudari* (Chennai, India: CLS, 2004), 109.

21 Ratna Sundara Rao Rayi, *Telugulo Chraistava Sahityam* (Chennai, India: Rayi Foundation, 2016), 17–35. Citing Sudha Ratnajali, Ranjit Kumar Kanithi classifies Chowdhari's songs into thirteen types. See also Sudha Ratnanjali Samuel, *Purshothama Chowdari Jeevitha Charitra* (Chennai, India: CLS, 1997), 73.

22 *Andhra Chraistava Keertanalu* [Andhra Christian hymnal] (n.p.: privately published by K. Matthew Henry, 2014).

23 Richard Lovett, *The History of the London Missionary Society, 1795–1895* (London: Henry Frowde, 1899), 2:130. See also Eustace B. Bromley, *They Were Men Sent from God: A Centenary Record (1836–1936) of Gospel Work in India amongst Telugus in the Godavari Delta and Neighbouring Parts* (Bangalore, India: Scripture Literature Press, 1937), 54.

illustrate the impact of the Brahminical worldview on the
Telugu Christian thought.

### Dalits Embrace Christianity

Even while the missionaries were preoccupied looking for dominant caste Hindus and the Brahmin converts were occupied
in shaping the Telugu Christian theology, Dalits converted
to Christianity in groups in the second half of the nineteenth
century, significantly altering the social fabric of the Telugu
Church.[24] The cultural resources Dalits brought with them in
many ways transformed the texture of Telugu Christianity. Protestant missionaries, who earlier valued individual conversions of
caste Hindus, had yielded to the notion of group conversions.[25]
This yielding was not without resistance, as missionaries time
and again doubted the authenticity of the seeker's conversion
experience—interior and personal—and refused to baptize.
Dalit preachers—women and men—traversed their hamlets
and brought interested families for baptism. As a result, Christianity had become a religion of the Dalits, a community faith
with social ramifications.

In addition to improvising their own, Dalits in the past
embraced and appropriated alien worldviews to meet their
social and religious needs. They formed or followed eclectic
movements. Peraiah Yerraguntla, who led thousands of Madigas to faith in Christ, had earlier followed Shaivite Hinduism, a

---

24  Hugald Grafe, *The History of the Work of the Hermannsburg Mission and
    Evangelical Lutheran Mission (ELM) for the South Andhra Lutheran Church (SALC)*
    (Chennai, India: Inter-Church Service Association Books, 2010), 16–17.
    Located in Tirupati and recognizing the futility of investing their time,
    German Lutherans focused on landowning communities.
25  John Clough, *Social Christianity in the Orient: The Story of a Man, a Mission
    and a Movement* (New York: Macmillan, 1914).

faith alien to his community.[26] The religious experiences in this tradition seem to have shaped his faith as a Christian.

Madigas also welcomed gurus from other communities. The Raja Yogi movement, an eclectic tradition founded by Potuluri Veerabrahmam, attracted the community. Characterized as a messianic movement, the Raja Yogi tradition preached social and gender equality and promised an impending alternative social order. In the movement, every follower despite their gender and social location could be a priest, a feature most likely to appeal to Dalits and women. Although Veerabrahmam was not a Dalit himself, most of his followers were.[27] According to Emma Rauschenbusch-Clough, an American Baptist missionary-anthropologist, these associations with alien religions prepared Peraiah and his Madiga community to align with Christianity.[28]

Relegated to the social margins, Dalits skillfully created myths to incorporate the dominant worldviews into their religious practice. The story of Matangi, a Dalit goddess, testifies to these efforts. Matangi was a fusion of a caste head and outcaste body.[29] According to the story from the Ongole district, Renuka, the wife of sagacious Jamadagni Bhagavan, went to bathe and fetch water for her husband's rituals in the Gundlakamma River early in the morning. A Dalit female bodyguard accompanied her. Lord Vishnu tricked her and appeared as Karthaviriyarjuna (the lord of vigor), also known as Gandharva, a warrior with a thousand arms. Attracted to a man besides her pious husband, Renuka lost her skill of rolling water into a pot-like water cube

26  Emma Rauschenbusch-Clough, *While Sewing Sandals: Tales of a Telugu Pariah Tribe*, rev. ed. (New Delhi: Asian Educational Services, 2000), 123.

27  Rauschenbusch-Clough, 123.

28  Rauschenbusch-Clough, 123. See also Clough, *Social Christianity*, 145.

29  Edgar Thurston, *Castes and Tribes of Southern India* (Madras, India: Government Press, 1909), 4:302. Dalits identify their goddess Ellamma also as the wife of Siva.

that morning. Sensing her deviance and enraged at the lack of water, the sage ordered their son Parashurama to slay his mother. Instead of murdering his mother, Parashurama killed the Madiga woman, his mother's bodyguard. Bhagavan was furious. He ordered his son to undo his mistake by beheading his mother. Parashurama dutifully killed his mother to placate his father. Pleased with his son's obedience, the father offered him any boon he wished for. The grieving son asked for the reanimation of his mother and was given life-giving waters. Delighted, Parashurama made another mistake. He hastily put his mother's head on the body of the Madiga woman. While the one with his mother's head became Renuka, the one with the Madiga head became Matangi. Dalits worship both victims but give more importance to Matangi. Most of the Dalit sacred stories incorporate portions of Vishnavite mythologies.

A variant of the legend portrays Matangi as an incarnation of Parvati, a victim of Siva. According to the legend, Goddess Parvati tricked Lord Siva. When Siva wanted her sexual favors, she refused, teased him, and escaped into an anthill. Furious at her refusal and wanting to kill her, Siva pierced his spear into the anthill and broke open her head. Parvati died and resurrected, holding heaven in her left hand and the great serpent Adishesha in her right hand.[30] She married Siva again and with him birthed five children. Parashurama, one of her sons, eventually beheaded her, causing her transformation into Matangi. This variant illustrates Dalits' encounter with Shaivite tradition and their willingness to incorporate it into their mythology.

These above-mentioned renderings of the goddess story reveal Dalits' ability to build social bridges through mythmaking. They also show their ability to subvert the sacred stories of the dominators and show the divine in victims. As mentioned later,

---

30  Wilber Theodor Elmore, *Dravidian Gods in Modern Hinduism: A Study of the Local and Village Deities of Southern India* (Hamilton, NY: privately published by the author, 1915), 94.

Dalits retained this accent on victim-god when they embraced the crucified Christ but had to abandon their goddesses.

As John C. B. Webster, a social historian, avers, Dalit conversions to Christianity were initiated by Dalits themselves.[31] Given the social stratification, these were a result of a decision taken by a social group or a cluster of families in a caste community.[32] Before inviting missionaries to baptize them, Dalits heard of Christianity, and finding it relevant to their aspirations—political and spiritual—they introduced it to their kin. With a desire to learn more, they then approached Christian missionaries and asked to be initiated into Christianity.

## What Else Was Happening?

Multiple factors contributed to mass conversions. First, the primary impetus for change came from Dalit experiences of bondage and slavery. The landowning communities on the subcontinent denied Dalits a share in the land, extracted their labor in production, and deprived them of a voice in the social life of the community. They legitimized and buttressed this exploitative socioeconomic system with religious resources. Seeking freedom from the stigma of untouchability and forced labor, Dalits have evolved belief systems that anthropologists call folk religions or popular expressions of Hinduism. As M. N. Srinivas points out, some of them subscribed to the purity norms and practices of the dominant groups to climb the social ladder.[33] Many Dalits allied with religions such as Islam and Buddhism. The availability of alternative worldviews and the volatile political situation of the mid-nineteenth century contributed to their conversions.

---

31  Webster, *Dalit Christians*, 70.
32  Jarrell W. Pickett, *Christian Mass Movements in India: A Study with Recommendations* (New York: Abingdon, 1933), 22.
33  Srinivas, *Social Change*, 7.

Second, the economy of the Telugus was based on agriculture, and so was the caste system. As mentioned earlier, the fecundity of the land necessitates the need for human labor, and the greed for profit results in the extraction of Dalit labor. On the contrary, excessive rains, abnormal seasons, and occasional droughts disrupt the "normal" social balance. They weaken landowners' control and provide bargaining opportunities for Dalits. Droughts destabilize faith in the belief systems that justify the caste system. With several serious famines between the 1930s and the 1970s, the agriculture-based Telugu society may have opened up sufficient fissures for the disenfranchised to challenge the status quo.[34]

Third, the British colonial officials with evangelical sympathies used their political influence to encourage missionary activities in the nineteenth century. A series of charters made this possible. First, the Charter Act of 1813 relaxed the rule against allowing missionaries to enter into the subcontinent.[35] Earlier, the East India Company was reluctant to allow the missionaries entrance, lest their interference with the native religions hurt their business interests. Second, with the Charter Act of 1833, the British Parliament legalized the East India Company's occupation of the Indian subcontinent and claimed the right to interfere in the social life of the locals.[36] This act also shifted power from governors-general to colonial administrators at the local level. Taking advantage of the changed political situation, some colonial officials encouraged compatriots to missionize in the region. A few others gathered congregations themselves and either handed them over to the Protestant missionaries or became missionaries. For example, William Howell,

---

34 Bromley, *Men Sent from God*, 36.

35 V. Ramakrishna, *Social Reform in Andhra: 1848–1919* (New Delhi, India: Vikas, 1983), 50.

36 The British East India Company issued a charter in 1833 permitting missionary activities in its colonies.

an Anglo-Indian surveyor in the Public Works Department in Kadapa, gathered a group of pious Europeans in 1822. He approached the LMS for a missionary. Later that year, instead of sending one, the LMS appointed Howell as its missionary. To strengthen his Anglican connections, Howell later asked the Society for the Propagation of the Gospel (SPG) to ordain him as a minister in 1942.[37] The beginnings of Anglicanism in Rayalaseema date back to the Howells.

Invited by the colonial agents in Machilipatnam, John Vesey Parnell, a Scottish Brethren missionary, arrived in 1836.[38] William Bowden and George Beers, English Brethren missionaries, followed. They moved to Narasapuram and established what was later named Godavari Delta Mission (GDM). Anthony Norris Groves—who invited Parnell, Bowden, and Beers to the region—moved to Chittoor in 1837.[39] Despite their theological differences, the British civil and military officers continued to fund the Brethren missionaries in their "faith" mission.[40] When the Brethren moved out of Machilipatnam, John Goldingham, Esq., collector of the Krishna district, and his pious colleagues approached the SPG and the CMS for a missionary in 1836.[41] The SPG and the CMS initially declined the request. Goldingham subsequently raised a sum of 21,841 rupees and formed the Telugu Missionary Society, which was a lifeline for

37 *Missionary Magazine and Chronicle* 17 (1839): 194. See Norman Goodall, *A History of the London Mission Society: 1895–1945* (London: Oxford University Press, 1954).
38 Bromley, *Men Sent from God*, 33. John Vesey Parnell was later named Lord Congleton.
39 Robert B. Dann, *Father of Faith Missions: The Life and Times of Anthony Norris Groves* (London: Authentic Media, 2004), 238.
40 Harold H. Rowdon, *The Origins of the Brethren, 1825–1850* (London: Pickering & Inglis, 1967), 198.
41 John Bob Williams, *A Study of the Economic Status and Self-Support of the Church of the Four Protestant Missions in the Andhra Area* (Guntur, India: Andhra Christian College, 1938), 5.

the Brethren until 1841, when the CMS missionaries Robert T. Noble and Henry W. Fox arrived in Machilipatnam.

Some colonial officers had contributed to the activities of the missionaries. For example, Colonel Arthur Cotton in Rajahmundry and Collector William Stokes in Guntur supported the educational work of Lutheran missionaries.[42] Stokes had personally invited Father Hayer and provided transportation to start missionary work in Guntur in 1842.[43] He had designated nine acres of land to establish a Christian neighborhood, modeled after the praying towns of eighteenth-century America.[44]

Fourth, in the fissures created by the Sepoy Mutiny (1857) and the subsequent transfer of control from the East India Company to the queen and in the presence of missionaries, Dalits found opportunities to struggle for better social status. In the pretext of religious neutrality, the British queen relaxed restrictions on missionaries after the Sepoy Mutiny. The legal freedom and protections provided to the converts emboldened Dalits to identify themselves with Christianity.

Fifth, the education offered by the Christian missionaries and the nontraditional employment opportunities in the British raj encouraged Dalits to imagine new possibilities in life. Dalits traditionally were assigned agrarian or sanitary occupations in society. Their labor was expected in sowing and reaping during the relevant seasons or producing accessories needed in agricultural production. The social order of the dominant also expected them to clean the streets and toilets. They, especially Madigas, tanned leather and produced and played drums for cultic purposes. During the nineteenth century, the British administrators employed them as watchmen, messengers, and

---

42 George Drach and Calvin F. Kuder, *The Telugu Mission of the General Council of the Evangelical Lutheran Church in North America* (Philadelphia: General Council Publication House, 1914), 104.

43 Swavely, *One Hundred Years*, 8.

44 Drach and Kuder, *Telugu Mission*, 82.

skilled professionals in their establishments. The women trained in mission schools were hired as schoolteachers and nurses in mission and government-funded schools and clinics.

Finally, the cultural climate engineered by the marginalized on the subcontinent as well as in the Western Hemisphere prepared missionaries to be receptive to Dalit struggles. By the middle of the nineteenth century, the Protestant missionaries of British origins had already been active in the abolitionist or philanthropic movements with their evangelical compatriots. Meanwhile, the second wave of evangelical revivals in the 1830s heightened missionary interest and the democratic impulses among Protestants in the United States.[45] Struggles for the emancipation of the slaves in North America resulted in the American Civil War and the subsequent declaration of abolition. Missionaries— male and female—experienced the baptism of blood during those events and thus were prepared for similar struggles on the Indian subcontinent. Missionaries' openness to ally with the disenfranchised groups brought them closer to Dalits.

### Waves of Conversions

The earliest of the Dalit group conversions was in the 1840s. Under the leadership of Kola Atchamma, a Madiga woman, a group of Madigas in Palakollu embraced Christianity. Atchamma would have been aware of Christianity even before meeting the Brethren missionaries because of her relationship with a European colonial official.[46] William Bowden, the resident Plymouth Brethren missionary, was in Dowleswaram, preaching to the construction workers at the upcoming irrigation dam during the famine of 1847–48, and returned to

---

45 Patricia Hill, *The World Their Household: The American Woman's Foreign Mission Movement and Cultural Transformation, 1870–1920* (Ann Arbor: University of Michigan Press, 1985), 36–40.

46 Bromley, *Men Sent from God*, 66.

Palakollu only in 1849.[47] In his absence, Atchamma introduced Christianity to her community and gathered a group of Madiga converts.

Two group conversions among Malas followed: one in Kurnool and another in Raghavapuram. Both were led by Mala leaders, whom Protestant missionaries and colonial law enforcement officers viewed as criminals.[48] Akutu Nancharu, an inmate in the Kadapa jail, met William Howell, an SPG missionary, in 1851.[49] He asked Howell to send teachers to his community in Rudravaram. Teachers taught religion on Sundays and literacy on weekdays. After Nancharu's release from the jail and at the behest of other local teachers, Malas in the region converted to Christianity en masse.[50] Citing the census, Susan Billington Harper, a historian of religion, numbers 1,700 Christians and a thousand more inquirers between 1852 and 1870.[51] This

---

47  William T. Stunt, ed., *Turning the World Upside Down: A Century of Missionary Endeavour* (Bath, UK: Echoes of Service, 1972), 91. See also Frederick A. Tatford, *The Challenge of India: That the World May Believe* (Bath, UK: Echoes of Service, 1984), 5:98. Writing after more than a century later, Stunt identifies the congregation members as those of dominant castes. It is probable that Atchamma found a place to live in a Sudhra neighborhood, given her access to power centers. But it is highly unlikely that a Madiga woman and the one with a previous conjugal relationship with a European official would have continued to reside in a non-Dalit neighborhood. Stunt—who earlier lists two, one dominant caste man and another outcaste woman, as the first converts—might describe the congregation as that of dominant caste in his enthusiasm to find only caste converts in the region.

48  Susan Billington Harper, *In the Shadow of the Mahatma: Bishop V. S. Azariah and the Travails of Christianity in British India* (Grand Rapids, MI: Eerdmans, 2000), 183.

49  Harper, 183.

50  *Missionary Conference*, 2:221–22; Tom Hiney, *On the Missionary Trail: A Journey through Polynesia, Asia, and Africa with the London Missionary Society* (New York: Atlantic Monthly Press, 2000), 346.

51  Harper, *Shadow of the Mahatma*, 184.

group conversion marks the beginning of Dalit conversions in Rayalaseema.

Meanwhile, Venkayya Pagolu of Raghavapuram, another outlaw, met Thomas Young Darling, an India-born CMS missionary, at a fair in Vijayawada.[52] Having introduced the new religion and convinced his community to join Christianity, Venkayya invited Darling to baptize them, resulting in a group conversion of the Mala community in and around Raghavapuram in the late 1850s.

While the crime of Nancharu was not specifically named, the character of Venkayya was. Venkayya from Raghavapuram was portrayed as "the ring leader of a band of violent men" who earned a living by robbing travelers on the highways.[53] Protestant missionaries, in their zeal to underline the impact of evangelical Christianity on the lives of individual converts, often vilified a convert's former lifestyle as outrageously inappropriate. The more missionaries demonized a convert's past, the better it served to highlight their civilizing mission.

According to the mission reports, Venkayya, with his spiritual aspirations, followed a popular Hindu ideology and was critical of Brahminical Hinduism.[54] He heard about Christianity through a native preacher and was inquisitive about its relevance to his situation. While visiting a Mala community in Polasanipalli, a village adjacent to Raghavapuram, Venkayya noticed the change of lifestyle as a result of the people's conversion to Christianity.[55] The sources are silent about the changes except to mention that there was a church building.[56] Nor do

---

52  Paul, *Triumphs of His Grace*, 93.
53  G. Hibbert Ware, *Christian Missions in the Telugu Country* (London: SPG, 1912), 187. Cf. Frederick F. Gledstone, *The CMS Telugu Mission: Being a Short Account of the Hundred Years 1841–1941* (Mysore, India: Wesley, 1941), 19.
54  Paul, *Triumphs of His Grace*, 94.
55  Paul, 108.
56  Paul, 111.

missionary reports indicate the importance of this building in the life of the community. The sources mention that Venkayya owned a piece of land in his hamlet and donated a portion of it for a church building.[57] The community was determined to have a place of worship.[58] The church buildings (*gudi*) in the missionary era were often also schools (*badi*) during the week. Studying the Dalit conversions in Kadapa, Chandra Sekhar Chakali observes that this duo of gudi and badi opened up new power possibilities.[59] Dalits were denied access to temples and literacy. The possibility of having these, therefore, was an attraction. In their approach to the missionaries, Malas specifically requested a place of worship.[60]

Characterized as a seeker after religious "truth,"[61] Venkayya traveled beyond his hamlet. Highly critical of the religion of the dominant, he sought religious alternatives. Having been impressed by the changes in Polasanipalli, Venkayya returned to his hometown, Raghavapuram, and shared about what the new religion had done to the Malas in Polasanipalli. The Mala community in Raghavapuram deliberated on the idea of conversions to Christianity for three years. In the process, Venkayya and his community inquired about a Western missionary who would initiate them into Christianity and teach its basic tenets. Having heard about Darling, a group of Malas traveled seventy miles south to Vijayawada to meet him.

Venkayya went to a Hindu shrine on the banks of the Krishna River in Vijayawada during a Siva Ratri festival looking

---

57  Thomas Young Darling, *A Telugu Convert: The Story of P. Venkayya* (London: CMS, 1893), 21.

58  Paul, *Triumphs of His Grace*, 112.

59  Chandra Sekhar Chakali, "In Search of Touchable Body: Christian Mission and Dalit Conversions," *Religions* 10, no. 12 (2019): 7. See Rupa Viswanath, *The Pariah Problem: Caste, Religion, and the Social in Modern India* (New York: Columbia University Press, 2015), 85.

60  Paul, *Triumphs of His Grace*, 112.

61  Hibbert Ware, *Telugu Country*, 187.

for a Christian missionary. Many Christian missionaries of the day considered preaching at Hindu festivals strategic to reach Hindus and saw no offense in the gesture. Unable to locate a Christian preacher in the crowd of Hindu devotees, Venkayya approached a Brahmin priest. This chance encounter resulted in a religious debate. Such interfaith encounters between self-taught Dalits and learned Brahmin priests were not abnormal, especially in the colonial period.[62] Despite following alternative indigenous religious systems, Dalits were familiar with the belief systems and argumentative syntax of the Brahmins, the system responsible for their degradation. It did not take long for the Brahmin priest to recognize the unorthodox tone of Venkayya's query. The priest promptly pointed Venkayya to Darling. Convinced of Christianity's potential for his aspirations, Venkayya returned home and introduced Christianity to his community. Venkayya and his community then invited Darling to baptize them in Raghavapuram.[63] He, along with twenty-six members of the Mala community in Raghavapuram, was baptized in 1859. The Mala communities within the Krishna region thus forced the CMS missionaries to reconsider their strategy of focusing on dominant castes as propounded by their illustrious predecessor Robert T. Noble, who did not find Dalits worth Christianizing.

Venkayya and his community requested Darling to baptize them as a mark of initiation into Christianity. Like some of his contemporaries, Darling initially doubted the sincerity of their request. Local preachers Venkayya and Buddha Seshayya demonstrated their commitment to the new religion by acquiring

---

62 Orville E. Daniel, *Moving with the Times: The Story of Outreach from Canada into Asia, South America, and Africa* (Toronto: CBFMB, 1973), 47. The ability to debate with Brahmin men was a celebrated gift. See also a report from Mrs. Isaac Cannaday entitled "Meenakshi: The Bible Woman," *Lutheran Women's Work* 14, no. 3 (March 1921): 83–84.

63 Darling, *Venkayya*, 14.

literacy and memorizing large portions of Christian Scriptures, a convincing shift from their Dalit spirituality to a religion of the book.[64] Aided by women preachers, they provided the Mala families in the hamlet with necessary instruction in the Christian faith and prepared them for baptism, leading to a group conversion.

A brief narration of another much-celebrated group conversion is appropriate here. Peraiah Yerraguntla, a Madiga from Talakondapadu, heard of Christianity and introduced it to his community, resulting in a wave of group conversions. Disenchanted with his folk beliefs, Peraiah had earlier followed Shaivite gurus. In one of his travels to purchase leather, he met with Madiga Christians in Palakollu in 1862 and, on the way back home, met with Abraham Vongolu in Eluru.[65] Recognizing Peraiah's interest in Christianity, Abraham introduced him to F. N. Alexander, a CMS missionary. Respecting the principle of comity, Alexander advised Peraiah to meet American Baptist missionaries in Nellore, as Peraiah's hometown, Talakondapadu, was under the American Baptist "jurisdiction." The practice of comity divided the mission territories among the mission societies.[66] After returning home, Peraiah preached Christianity to his community and, with a group of potential converts, approached John Clough to initiate them into the Christian community. While Clough was hoping to Christianize individual souls from a Hindu background, Madigas stormed the mission bungalow asking for baptism.[67] When approached, Clough was not convinced about the sincerity of the inquirers' interests and refused to baptize them. Eventually,

64  Paul, *Triumphs of His Grace*, 112.
65  Clough, *Social Christianity*, 95; Bromley, *Men Sent from God*, 162.
66  Charlotte C. Wycoff, *A Hundred Years with Christ in Arcot: A Brief History of the Arcot Mission in India of the Reformed Church in America* (Madras, India: Ahura Press, 1953), 39.
67  Clough, *Social Christianity*, ix.

Clough yielded to the Madigas' pressure to baptize them as a group—once they began to negotiate with a Catholic missionary for baptism. The Madiga preachers, with the help of Clough, baptized thousands of Madigas in the summer of 1878.

Another group conversion followed in the northern districts of coastal Andhra. Marayya Taleru, alias Thomas Gabriel, introduced Christianity to Malas and invited Canadian Baptist missionaries to the Godavari districts. Marayya was a Mala from Gunnanipudi. Though he was born in a remote village, he grew up in the urban surroundings of Machilipatnam, where his father was a peon in the colonial courthouse. British colonial administrators offered Dalits nontraditional professions. He studied at an elementary school founded by the GDM and pursued high school at a Lutheran mission school.[68] Secondary education and connections with the colonial fraternity earned Marayya employment in the Department of Telegraphs in Dowleswaram.[69] In the colonial period, Dalits took advantage of the literacy offered by missionaries and nontraditional occupations provided by the colonial administrators. After a series of transfers and journeys, Marayya fell ill. During his illness, Marayya met Das Anthervedy, a Telugu Baptist chaplain in a British regiment, at a hospital in Chennai. Impressed by Anthervedy's preaching and piety, Marayya became a Baptist preacher.[70] After returning home in 1870, Marayya resigned from his government services and preached full-time to fellow Dalits in his hometown. He moved to Kakinada along with the Bowdens, a Plymouth Brethren missionary family. While

68  Craig et al., *Telugu Trophies*, 2.

69  Malcolm L. Orchard and Katherine S. McLaurin, *The Enterprise: The Jubilee Story of the Canadian Baptist Mission in India, 1874–1924* (Toronto: CBFMB, 1925), 174.

70  Mabel Evangeline Archibald, *Glimpses and Gleams of India and Bolivia: The Jubilee Book of Mission Bands* (Toronto: American Baptist Publication Society for Baptist Women's Missionary Societies of Canada, 1923), 112.

moving, he appointed his brother, Nathan Gabriel, as a local preacher in his hometown, Gunnanipudi, the same year. The Mala community in Gunnanipudi converted en masse in 1873.[71]

The "faith" model of the Brethren did not work in Marayya's mission. Inspired by the Pauline model of tent making, a practice the Brethren missionaries promoted, Marayya started a tannery in Kakinada. He had to feed not only his family but also the native preachers he appointed. Marayya's business faltered. So did his subsequent approach to the Strict Baptists of England in Chennai and the American Baptists in Nellore. He then approached John McLaurin, a Canadian Baptist missionary working as an auxiliary to the American Baptist Missionary Union in Ramayapatnam, in 1871 and invited him to Kakinada. Subsequently, the Canadian Baptist Foreign Mission Board (CBFMB) decided in 1873 to start a mission station at Kakinada independent of their American counterparts and appointed the McLaurins as missionaries.[72] The McLaurins joined Marayya in Kakinada in 1874. As a result of the mission activism of Marayya, more than two hundred Dalits embraced Christianity that same year.[73]

In all these cases, it was Dalits who heard about Christianity, deliberated on conversion, and invited Western missionaries to join their movement toward Christianity. There are at least four traits the named leaders shared: (1) They crossed the cultural boundaries of the Dalit worldview and were in contact with the outside world. While Venkayya and Peraiah followed neo-Hindu ideologies, Marayya attended a school and learned to write. (2) These leaders geographically crossed their community or village boundaries, unlike their Dalit contemporaries

71  Thomas S. Shenston, *Teloogoo Scrap Book* (Brantford, Ontario: Expositor Book and Jobs Office, 1888), 129.

72  Craig, *Among the Telugus*, 34.

73  Gordon W. Carder, *Hands to the Indian Plow* (Madras, India: CLS, 1976), 1:33.

who mostly limited their activities to ancestral villages. (3) They were acquainted with the cash economy. Venkayya's profession earned him income in cash, as did Marayya's working for the British East India Company. This was against the traditional economy, where Dalit's services were rewarded in kind, either in grains or in cloth. (4) They were open to allying with missionaries to help in their social and religious struggles.

Why did Dalits convert to Christianity? There is a myriad of factors that may have contributed to the group conversions of Malas and Madigas. First, postcolonial historians attribute conversion to the political conditions of the day, especially the transfer of power from the East India Company to the British queen after the failed Sepoy Mutiny in 1857.[74] The policy of religious neutrality indirectly ushered in Protestant missionaries with whom evangelical colonial officers collaborated actively. The changed political situation brought in laws that protected individual freedom to choose one's religion. While rightly acknowledging the disruption the empire caused in the Indian culture, this narrative downplays the agency of the convert in the conversions.

Second, the nationalist writers attribute mass conversions to famines and the relief activities that the missionaries undertook.[75] They portray converts as "rice Christians," or those who embraced an alien religion seeking material benefits. Although droughts and religious conversions coincided and may have had a connection, reducing the material benefits as the incentive for religious conversions and calling converts rice Christians do not account for the conversions that took place before the famines. For example, the first wave of Madiga conversions took place before the 1876–78 famine in the Ongole region

---

74  Gauri Viswanathan, *Outside the Fold: Conversion, Modernity and Belief* (Princeton: Princeton University Press, 1998), 213–14.

75  Arun Shourie, *Missionaries in India: Continuities, Changes, and Dilemmas* (New Delhi: HarperCollins, 1998), 7.

and the second only after the famine. The third, and the largest, group conversion took place long after the famine had ended.[76] The fourth one followed in 1890 despite the persecutions. In all these conversions, Dalits remained with Christianity at the risk of losing basic human amenities, such as food and water.

Third, social historians place the group conversions to Christianity in the context of broader Dalit struggles for social mobility.[77] According to them, religious conversion to Christianity is a social weapon that Dalits employed to free themselves from a religiously sanctioned servitude. Placed at the bottom of the Hindu caste hierarchy, Dalits wanted to assert their religious identity and escape the stigma of impurity in Hinduism. Non-Hindu religions offered that opportunity.

The above-mentioned interpretation by social historians explains why groups—marginalized and dominating—make religious decisions with social implications. It also recognizes the agency of the converting group. However, this interpretation ignores the decisions individual converts made despite the whims and dictates of the community. Some leaders in Dalit conversions embraced Christianity first as individuals before others in the community decided to join them. This interpretation does not account for the longing individual converts may have had in converting to Christianity. For example, Venkayya and Peraiah, spurred by their spiritual quests, affiliated with different religious groups before embracing Christianity. While it is reasonable to conclude that multiple factors, including the colonial backdrop and alliances with missionaries, contributed to the decisions of Dalits to become Christians, it is highly

---

76 Clough, *Social Christianity*, 263.

77 Webster, *Dalit Christians*; Dick Kooiman, *Conversion and Social Equality in India: The London Missionary Society in South Travancore in the 19th Century* (New Delhi, India: Manohar, 1989); Geoffrey Oddie, *Social Protest in India: British Protestant Missionaries and Social Reforms, 1850–1900* (New Delhi, India: Manohar, 1979); Viswanath, *Pariah Problem*.

probable that the social struggles of the groups and spiritual longings of individuals together spurred Dalit conversions to Christianity.

Meanwhile, group conversions of Dalits to Christianity were not limited to the Protestant churches. A series of mass conversions began in the coastal districts at the dawn of the twentieth century. Solomon Thanugundla records one such in the Krishna district in 1911.[78] Dalit communities from eleven villages in the district requested to be admitted into the Catholic Church.[79] According to Solomon, the Dalit conversions were so pervasive that by 1935, at least fourteen of the seventeen priests in the Visakhapatnam diocese were Dalits.[80] Dalit communities joined the Roman Catholic Church in Telangana around the same period.[81]

### What Did They Mean?

In these group conversions, religious conversion signaled the change of religious identity. It differed from the missionaries' notions of conversion as an interior experience of an individual. It was also a slight variant of the process of Sanskritization. In Christianization, Malas and Madigas opted out of the dominant system, whereas in Sanskritization, they would have had to negotiate with the Brahminical system.

In their "adoption" of their Christian identities, Dalits did not abandon their community identities and cultural roots.[82] Emma Rauschenbusch-Clough, a Baptist missionary, describes

---

78 Thanugundla, *Structures*, 197.
79 Carlo Toriani, *History of PIME in Andhra* (Eluru, India: PIME, 2005), 87.
80 Thanugundla, *Structures*, 213.
81 Toriani, *History of PIME*, 111.
82 Duncan N. Forrester, *Caste and Christianity: Attitudes and Policies on Caste of Anglo-Saxon Protestant Missions in India* (London: Curzon, 1980), 77.

the Madiga conversion in Ongole as "uniting" with Christians.[83] Convinced of Christianity's relevance for his quest,
Peraiah told his people that he would join "the people of the
Christian sect."[84] Rauschenbusch-Clough explains that this
"uniting" did not uproot the community from its pre-Christian
roots and community bonds. They retained their social cohesion even while seeking to affiliate with missionaries.[85]

Conversion ensured social cohesion. The community elders
became the deacons in the local congregations.[86] They oversaw
matters of discipline, worship, and administration. The ministry of a deacon also included social activism in times of "social
uprisings."[87] The deacons were the cashiers, accountants, and
supervisors at the Buckingham Canal construction project,
which Clough undertook during the drought years of 1876–78.
Madiga deacons' involvement in the canal construction work
broadened the scope of their ministry and included public life
as part of the diaconate.

Conversion also entailed some cultural alternations. While
some may have retained the practices of drinking alcohol and
eating the meat of dead animals, most Madiga Christians in
Ongole refused to work on Sundays and play drums before the
village deities.[88] These practices may have had their origins in
the nineteenth-century evangelical tradition of North America, which viewed temperance and "cleanliness" to be essential marks of a "regenerated" Christian. However, by refusing
to clean the carrion from the village and to work on Sundays,
Dalit Christians were challenging their landlords.

---

83  Rauschenbusch-Clough, *While Sewing Sandals*, 97.
84  Rauschenbusch-Clough, 97.
85  Rauschenbusch-Clough, ix.
86  Clough, *Social Christianity*, 192.
87  Clough, 192.
88  Clough, 161–67.

As mentioned earlier, religious conversion has been one of the many weapons that Dalits employed in their search for social dignity. For example, Madigas in Ongole had earlier aligned themselves with "messianic" movements led by Nasraiah[89] and Potuluri Veerabrahmam.[90] Stephen Fuchs categorized these movements as "messianic" movements because of their vision of social equality and freedom.[91] Madigas eventually preferred Christianity to these movements probably due to the growing sense of social alienation they experienced within the movements. There were power struggles within Nasraiah's movement despite its egalitarian precepts and Madigas' enthusiastic participation.[92] Nasraiah himself felt insecure due to the growing influence of Madigas in his movement.[93]

In the Western missionary, Dalits found an ally who would facilitate their access to colonial power. In her brilliant analysis of the struggles of the Dalits in the northern districts of Tamil Nadu at the dawn of the twentieth century, Rupa Viswanath, a social historian, characterizes Dalit conversions as a political alliance with the Western missionaries.[94] Denied a right to own land, acquire literacy, and be free from the centuries-old servitude, Tamil Dalits collaborated with Christian missionaries.

---

89  This is a Dalit rendering of Nasr Mohammed Mastan. He is believed to have been a rich Muslim who renounced his wealth in favor of becoming a poor religious teacher. Nasr denounced image worship and preached social and gender equality. I identify him as Nasraiah in this book, as his Madiga followers called him so.

90  Potuluri Veerabrahmam predicted a millennial rule of social justice and peace. His life and message resemble that of Jesus. Veerabrahmam is believed to have brought forth life out of the dead and promised his coming reign.

91  Stephen Fuchs, *Rebellious Prophets: A Study of Messianic Movements in Indian Religions* (Bombay, India: Asia Publishing House, 1965), 260–63.

92  Rauschenbusch-Clough, *While Sewing Sandals*, 166.

93  Alvin T. Fishman, *Culture Change and the Underprivileged: A Study of Madigas in South India under Christian Guidance* (Madras, India: CLS, 1941), 11.

94  Vishwanath, *Pariah Problem*, 89.

Religious conversion thus was a political strategy. Although it may not account for the spiritual fulfillment Dalits found in conversion, one can discern the political motives in Telugu Dalits' conversion to Christian. For example, the sight of Clough on a horse, often identifiable with colonial power, is said to have excited the converts.[95] Owning a horse symbolized power, and the Madiga preachers saw Clough as a symbol of power in their struggles against the Hindu oppressors. Clough secured a contract to construct a dam from the colonial government, which was the mainstay for Dalits during the famine of 1786.

### Impact on Christianity

As a result of these mass conversions, the church grew 100 percent in the second half of the nineteenth century, estimates Stephen Neill, a bishop and mission historian.[96] Overall, the pace and enormity of these conversions were so extensive that Jarrell W. Pickett, a Methodist bishop, entitled his analysis of the conversions *Christian Mass Movements in India*.[97] Not only did the Telugu Church grow numerically, but it had also become a Dalit church. Given the nature of conversion, each congregation could be identified with one of the two Dalit communities. The rivalries among the Dalits forbade members from rival communities from joining.[98]

Religious conversion also enabled Dalits to highlight the social dimension of the Christian faith. Dalit Christians retained their pre-Christian understanding of religion as inseparable from the social life of the community. Religious experience

---

95  Clough, *Social Christianity*, 174.

96  Neill, *History of Christian Missions*.

97  Pickett, *Christian Mass Movements*.

98  Grafe, *Hermannsburg Mission*, 20. Cf. F. Colyer Sackett, *Out of the Miry Clay: The Story of the Haidarabad Mission to the Outcastes* (London: Wesleyan Methodist Missionary Society, 1924), 38.

is communitarian. Rauschenbusch-Clough describes this Dalit Christianity as "Social Christianity in the Orient."[99] Indeed, this distinct form of Christianity opened Clough's eyes to the possibilities of Christianizing the social structures.

We see a parallel tradition in the Social Gospel movement in North America. It was not a mere coincidence that there were several connections between the two. Clough made a decisive impact on the intellectual journey of Walter Rauschenbusch and thereby potentially in the inception of the Social Gospel tradition. Barbara A. Lundsten suggests that Clough, with his mission experiences, sowed the seeds of social Christianity in Rauschenbusch when he preached a convocation sermon at Rochester Theological Seminary, where Rauschenbusch was a student.[100] Paul W. Harris, a Baptist historian, identifies the connections between these two movements but credits Rauschenbusch-Clough, sister of Walter Rauschenbusch, for kindling social consciousness in Clough.[101] Dalitized Christianity in Ongole and the Social Gospel tradition in North America served as a two-way street for theological thought.

The preachers, who once were religious teachers in their pre-Christian lives, lived at the mercy of their congregations, just as a Hindu guru or Raja Yogi would. Although the local preachers hesitated to receive the monthly salary and depended on native Christians, they did not refuse the monetary "help" offered by John Clough. Madiga preachers' willingness to receive quarterly "help" had a symbolic value. It reflects their alliance with Clough, as Madigas viewed him as a liaison between them and

---

99  Clough, *Social Christianity*.

100  Barbara A. Lundsten, "The Legacy of Walter Rauschenbusch: A Life Informed by Mission," *International Bulletin of Missionary Research* 28 (April 2004): 75–78.

101  Paul W. Harris, "The Social Dimensions of Foreign Missions: Emma Rauschenbusch and Social Gospel Ideology," in *Gender and the Social Gospel* (Urbana: University of Illinois Press, 2003), 91.

the British colonial officers. Aligning with Clough not only increased their bargaining power with the local Hindu masters but also promised security in case of persecution. Madigas would have viewed this alliance as a status symbol and weapon in their power struggles. When Clough became bankrupt and could not continue to pay the quarterly remuneration, Madiga preachers preferred that he stop giving them quarterly "help" rather than sell his horse.

When faced with a dilemma of choosing between enthusiastic Dalits and interested Hindus, it was claimed that Clough aimlessly wandered among the biblical pages and miraculously found the verses 1 Corinthians 1:26–29, in which Paul reminds the reader about God's preference for the weak and the socially despised.[102] His first wife, Harriet S. Clough, also was said to have been led to these verses. However, we can infer that the praxis of the Madiga faith forced a U-turn (*metanoia*) in Clough's missionary ideology and gave him a new canon of biblical texts to guide his interaction with the poor. It was an ideological conversion for Clough as he began to believe that the gospel was God's gift for the weak and the despised in society.

Documenting her husbands' memoirs, Rauschenbusch-Clough offers a few clues on the themes that dominated Madigas' sermons. She recollects the aspects of Jesus's mission—healing, loving, and feeding—that characterized native god talk. Dalit preachers were said to have told and retold the stories of Jesus as one who healed the sick, loved little children, and fed the hungry.[103] Rauschenbusch-Clough claims that the emphasis on the physical, social, and emotional aspects of Jesus's ministry had

---

102  Herbert Waldo Hines, *Clough: Kingdom-Builder in South India* (Philadelphia: Judson, 1929), 78.

103  Clough, *Social Christianity*, 249.

sunk into Dalits' minds.[104] She relates that Madiga preachers repeatedly read Jesus's call "Come unto me, all ye that labor and are heavy-laden, and I will give rest" during the famine years, 1876–78, and hungry workers were drawn to this invitation.[105] In his historical fiction written at the dusk of the twentieth century, G. Kalyana Rao, a social activist, captures the appeal the Christian message had for the Dalits.[106] Although it is hard to rely on Rauschenbusch-Clough's representation of the native god-talk given her agenda and theological orientation, it does not surprise me, as this portrait of Jesus has been and continues to be the hallmark of Dalit preaching.[107] Given the agenda of Madigas' conversions to Christianity, experiences of subjugation, and oppositions to caste inequalities, Madiga preachers would not have abandoned Nasraiah's teachings about social equality and freedom. Madigas' choices to cite biblical instructions on the Sabbath and "idol worship" to defy their oppressors reflect how they recovered the subversive nature of the gospel.

The influx of Dalits in the Telugu Church significantly changed the texture of Christianity in the region. Dalits helped recover the civil dimensions and social utility of the Christian faith. Despite the shift in demographical changes, dominant caste Christians, with their literary gifts and access to the pulpit,

---

104 Clough, 249. G. Kalyana Rao reconstructs this aspect in his historical fiction *Antarani vasantham* [Untouchable spring] (Hyderabad, India: Viplava Rachayitala Sangham, 2000).

105 Rauschenbusch-Clough, *While Sewing Sandals*, 281.

106 Kalyana Rao, *Antarani vasantham*.

107 Harris argues that Rauschenbusch-Clough represents this Christianity as social Christianity using the ideological lens of her brother, Walter Rauschenbusch, the founder of the Social Gospel tradition in North America. One can also argue that the ideology of Theosophy, to which Rauschenbusch-Clough converted by the time she wrote her book *Social Christianity in the Orient* (which Rauschenbusch-Clough wrote but attributed to John Clough, as he had narrated the story to her), might have blurred her representation.

continued to dominate the processes of translating the Christian message. Women of Dalit and caste origins, with their traditional spheres of influence and access to families, shaped Telugu Christianity. Our understanding of Telugu Christianity would be incomplete without paying attention to the ways women impacted the faith and piety of Telugu Christianity. We shall move to these ways now.

# 4

# Women's Leadership in the Making of Telugu Christianity

The studies in the past on the history of Christianity in India often focused on either the Western missionaries or the native male church leaders. The scarce voices that studied native women often highlighted the conversion and ministries of celebrated Brahmin women, such as Pandita Ramabai and Chandra Leela.[1] In her groundbreaking essay, Evangeline Bharathi Nuthalapati draws our attention to the Telugu women, especially to those at the social margins, and analyzes their encounters with missionary Christianity in Machilipatnam.[2] She astutely identifies the predicament local women found themselves in because of "colonial-missionary collusion, the fetters of caste, patriarchy and their mindset."[3] Meanwhile, Eliza Kent studies the case of Tamil Biblewomen, while Mrinalini Sebastian examines the practices of Kannada Biblewomen, both focusing on

---

1 Agnes E. Baskerville, *Radiant Lights and Little Candles: Being a Group of Stories of Indian Characters for Children* (n.p., 1985), 7–11. See also Thomas, *100 Indian Witnesses*, 22–23.

2 Evangeline Bharathi Nuthalapati, "Women's Predicament as They Encountered Christianity: A Case Study of C.M.S. Telugu Mission in Andhra," *Indian Church History Review* 35, no. 2 (December 2001): 147–67.

3 Nuthalapati, 155.

how these native women negotiated tradition, modernity, and empire.[4]

Gratefully following their lead and recognizing the dearth of resources, I have attempted to study the theologies and history of Telugu Biblewomen, especially those of Lutheran and Baptist backgrounds in the coastal districts of Andhra Pradesh. In my work, I have demonstrated how the Telugu women, especially the Biblewomen, took advantage of the opportunities that Protestant Christianity and the colonial context offered and how they shaped Telugu Christianity. Telugu Biblewomen introduced Protestant Christianity to their communities and modeled its piety. Reading the missionary sources further, I realize that Telugu female schoolteachers and nurses were also equally accessible to the communities and influential in teaching the Bible, interpreting the tradition, and modeling Christian piety. They also remained in constant contact with their non-Christian neighbors daily, living out their faith and contributing to the general ethos of Telugu society. In their pre-Christian worldviews, Telugu women were accustomed to leading their families and communities in matters of faith. Evangelical Christianity—with its foci on Scriptures, literacy, and health—opened additional opportunities. In doing so, women transformed and shaped the texture of Telugu Christianity. In this chapter, I will analyze how Telugu Biblewomen, schoolteachers, and nurses led the nascent church in the late nineteenth and the first half of the twentieth centuries.

## Women in Local Cultures

As mentioned earlier, Telugu culture was homogenous with multiple communities, each with its own subculture. The place of

---

4 Mrinalini Sebastian, "Reading Archives from a Postcolonial Feminist Perspective: 'Native' Bible Women and the Missionary Ideal," *Journal of Feminist Studies in Religion* 19, no. 1 (Spring 2003): 5–25.

women in each community varied, as did their roles in transmitting and safeguarding their worldviews. For example, Dalit women traditionally held relatively more ritual power than their counterparts in caste communities. It may not have always and necessarily translated into the social sphere.[5] With some exceptions, women's places within the caste communities were slightly different. The higher the ranking of a social group, the more oppressive it was to its women.

In rural settings where agriculture was the primary source of income, Dalit women labored along with men to make ends meet. Women's labor did not guarantee them an equal share in their families' decision-making, but the abilities to move beyond their homes and be a part of their family economies provided Dalit women with a relatively better status compared to their counterparts in caste communities—at least before their conversion to Christianity and subsequent Sanskritization.

At the symbolic level, goddesses dominated the Dalit pantheon. Dalits worshipped goddesses, such as Maramma, Poleramma, Poshamma, Gonthi, Ellamma, Kaamma, Morasamma, Matangi (Mathamma), Somalamma, and Moosamma.[6] Dalits looked up to these deities in times of need and calamity. They not only worshipped goddesses but goaded the landlords to offer libations to them at the times of sowing and harvest. With an implicit conviction that the land belonged to the local goddess and that anyone tilling the land needed divine permission, their non-Dalit neighbors, regardless of their caste, placated the presiding (Dalit) deity during the times of threshing corn, building new houses, or

---

5  Elmore, *Dravidian Gods*, 29–31; P. Y. Luke and John B. Carman, *Village Christians and Hindu Culture* (London: Lutterworth, 1968), 57; Sackett, *Vision and Venture*, 117.

6  Elmore lists seven goddesses, or seven sisters, whom Dalits and Sudhras alike worshipped in the Nellore district. They are Poleramma, Ankamma, Muthyalamma, Dilli Polasi, Bangaramma, Mathamma, and Renuka. Elmore, *Dravidian Gods*, 19–28.

opening newly dug wells.[7] This belief subtly drew the landowning communities to join Dalits in the worship of their goddesses. The popular beliefs that the land belonged to the native goddesses and that the Dalit priestess represented the deity may have been the implicit cause for this unlikely alliance between the Dalit communities and the landowning castes.

At the ritual level, Dalit women priests, by and large, led their male counterparts.[8] Through oracles, they represented the deity. Matangi, a Madiga priestess named after the goddess, represented the latter.[9] She presided at the purificatory ceremonies that preceded all village feasts and festivals.[10] During appointed seasons of a year, she led ritual processions, visiting every street in the village and entering caste houses at her will. During her march, she abused caste landlords and spat on them, a gesture that the social elite considered to be purifying.[11]

Dalit priestesses uttered divine oracles, often prescribing remedies for the epidemics or famines that plagued villages. John Carman, a historian of religion and a Baptist missionary, described a ritual during which a Kolpula woman transmitted

---

7   For more about this, please see James Elisha Taneti, *Caste, Gender, and Christianity in Colonial India: Telugu Women in Mission* (New York: Palgrave Macmillan, 2013), 28–30.

8   Elmore, *Dravidian Gods*, 70; Henry Whitehead, *Village Gods of South India* (New York: Oxford University Press, 1916), 63.

9   While male priests inherit their office, a Madiga woman becomes a Matangi when chosen by the deity through possession and endorsed by the village community after a series of tests. A female priestess in the cult of Nukalamma inherits the office from her mother. Thurston, *Castes and Tribes*, 4:295. See also Joyce Burkhalter Flueckiger, "Wandering from 'Hills to Alleys' with the Goddess: Protection and Freedom in the *Matamma* Tradition of Andhra," in *Women's Lives, Women's Rituals in the Hindu Tradition*, ed. Tracy Pintchman (New York: Oxford University Press, 2007), 35–54.

10  Thurston, *Castes and Tribes*, 4:295–305.

11  Elmore, *Dravidian Gods*, 25.

the oracles from the cholera goddess.[12] The role of male priests
was limited to invoking the goddess through their drums and
killing sacrificial animals. A woman, on the other hand, typically
served as an intermediary between the deity and her village.
Thus the religious systems that Dalit groups had evolved and
promoted among the socially dominant provided more space
for women.

The status of women among the caste communities was
much more complex and ambivalent. Again, it would be highly
inaccurate to characterize their status, as there were numerous
subgroups among Hindus. Caste women may have been active
in farm and household leadership but were not allowed to venture out to minimize their possible interactions with men of
other communities. The gold they inherited from their mothers
and maternal ancestors was their primary economic bargaining tool. Dowries and other assets brides brought at the time
of their weddings became the properties of their husbands. By
and large, men were the heirs to the family properties, and protection of the properties and the "purity of the castes" were
safeguarded through arranged marriages.

In the Shaivite tradition, both men and women undertook
pilgrimages, offered pujas at the temple, and observed ritual baths
and weekly fasts. Being closely connected to children, women
were the transmitters of the tradition. In the bhakti tradition,
an outgrowth of Vaishnavism, goddesses were subservient to
gods, but this worldview allowed women prominent roles in
interpreting and transmitting the tradition both in public and
in family spheres.[13] The Dalit goddesses, such as Gonthelamma,
were negative reflections of their counterparts in Hindu mythology. The Hindu epics villainized Kunti, but Dalits deified her.
The interpretive lens and agenda of the community played

---

12  Luke and Carman, *Village Christians*, 57.
13  The bhakti tradition is prominent within Hinduism.

critical parts every time an epic was retold in or by a community. While rerendering epics, such as Ramayana, Telugu Dalits mitigated the status between gods and goddesses.

These interpretative processes of the tradition mirror the places women occupied in each community. As custodians of the tradition, Hindu and Dalit women retained Sanskritic goddesses, but as catalysts of change, Dalit women reinterpreted these deities. In doing so, women of both communities claimed a certain amount of agency in their cultural changes and carried these roles into Christianity.

### Telugu Women and Western Missionaries

The missionary movement the Telugu women encountered was a movement of the women. With the founding of female seminaries, women in the North Atlantic world found missionary careers abroad attractive and recognized that marrying an outgoing male missionary was a helpful strategy to accomplish their missionary callings. For example, Mount Holyoke Female Seminary in the United States was considered a "rib factory" for training women who would accompany male missionaries as wives.[14] At the seminary, mission societies and the seminary administration scouted brides for male missionaries destined to go abroad to connect them with their students.

With the opportunities to engage in roles traditionally beyond theirs during the Civil War and lessons learned from the experience, American women were ready to make an impact beyond their households, and some beyond their national boundaries. While some interpret this interest as a willingness to be "useful" in God's household, other feminists find social

---

14  Clifton Johnson, *Old-Time and School-Books* (New York: Macmillan, 1904), 146.

aspirations in women's eagerness to make their households.[15] During the Civil War, a considerable number of American women had acquired the skills necessary to act publicly. While men were away, engaged in combat, women led their families and communities. After the war, women looked for opportunities to continue their leadership in public life, and foreign missions provided an ideal opportunity to do that. As a result, in the decade following the Civil War, five Presbyterian, four Baptist, three Congregational, and two Methodist women's mission boards emerged.[16] Across the border, Canadian women were eager to join their American counterparts abroad, feminizing the missionary workforce on the Indian subcontinent.

With this interest in missionary work among women and perhaps due to the dearth of interested men or out of a desire to be autonomous, many joined the missionary force as single-women missionaries, substantially increasing the number of women at mission stations. Baptist missionary Lavinia Peabody, a Mount Holyoke alumna, was the first single-woman missionary to arrive among the Telugus. She reached Nellore in 1871, followed by Emma Rauschenbusch-Clough, an alum of Rochester Female Seminary, three years later. Kate Boggs was the first Lutheran single-woman missionary. She arrived in 1881, followed by Anna Sarah Kugler two years later. Due to illness, Boggs returned the same year. Agnes I. Schade and Amy S. Sadtler joined the Lutheran missionaries in Andhra in 1890.

The steep increase in women among missionary personnel could be seen in the female-male ratios in the mission

---

15  Dana Robert, *American Women in Mission: A Social History of Their Theory and Practice* (Macon, GA: Mercer University Press, 1984), 417; Hill, *World Their Household*, 36–40; Ruth C. Brouwer, *New Women for God: Canadian Presbyterian Women and India Missions, 1876–1914* (Toronto: University of Toronto Press, 1990), 18.

16  Hill, *World Their Household*, 13.

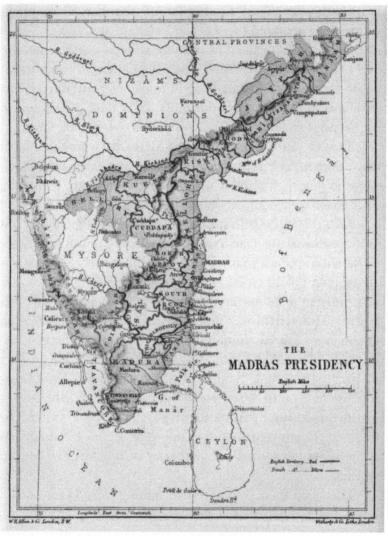

The Madras Presidency in the nineteenth century

Source: Map from the Imperial Gazetteer of India, new edition, held by
University of Chicago library. Courtesy of the Digital South Asia Library,
http://dsal.uchicago.edu.

compounds. For instance, there was one single-woman missionary in 1882 among Canadian Baptist missionaries, while there
were thirteen by 1906.[17] Among Lutheran missionaries, there were
two female single missionaries in 1890 compared to four missionary families—that is, the ratio of six women to four men.
By the end of the century, the number of single-women missionaries increased to seven, while the number of missionary
families was nine—that is, sixteen women and nine male missionaries.[18] While male missionaries itinerated accompanied
by the local preachers, these women missionaries invested their
skills and energies in hospitals, schools, and women.

The local conditions and cultures forced the missionaries
to reevaluate their goals and strategies. They had to improvise
their strategies and look for local allies. First, access to local
women was one of the primary challenges Western missionaries faced. The cultural taboos restricted access to native women
for any men other than their immediate family members. No
man—local or foreign—would ordinarily be trusted or welcomed to enter a house unless they were related to the host
family. Given their social location as foreigners and their per-
ceived ability to defile the host families, women missionaries
were not enthusiastically welcomed into the native homes, the
most likely possible meeting sites between women missionaries
and the Telugu women. Compared to their foreign missionary
counterparts, local converts could more easily access other local
women, who were crucial in disseminating the Christian message. Second, missionaries had undergone language learning,
but their limited knowledge of the vernacular hampered their
ability to communicate the Christian message to the natives.
Their local allies were better equipped to translate the gospel into Telugu cultural idioms. Third, missionaries were not

---

17 Craig, *Among the Telugus*, 217.
18 Drach and Kuder, *Telugu Mission*.

accustomed to the local temperature, which usually was intol-
erably hot most of the year. Many missionaries contracted ill-
nesses, and some even died due to their inability to cope with
the climate.[19] Confined to their bungalows due to the scorching
heat, missionaries depended on their local allies. Fourth, the
institutions that missionaries established and programs they
launched required more personnel than the missionaries had.
The local interlocutors were willing to collaborate with their
missionary allies. The local conditions demanded native collab-
orators. In their encounters with Christianity, Telugu women
saw not only a movement of the women but also opportunities
to collaborate with their counterparts from abroad.

### Biblewomen: "With Bibles in Hand"

Recognizing their limitations as well as the gifts and interest of
the local women, Protestant missionaries transported the office
of Biblewoman to the region. This profession has its origins
in the East End of London, where the British Bible and Foreign Society appointed Marion Bower, a working-class woman
of Irish descent, as Biblewoman in 1857.[20] Reporting to Ellen
Henrietta Ranyard, the founder of the London Bible and
Domestic Female Mission, Bowers traversed the streets in the
East End and taught the Bible, hygiene, and self-help skills to
the women there. Telugu women allied with women missionaries as Biblewomen and contextualized this lay ministerial office.

At work by 1869, Lydia, whose full name we do not know, may
have been the earliest appointee.[21] A native of Visakhapatnam
and a member of the LMS served in Nellore. It is likely that

---

19  Grafe, *Hermannsburg Mission*, 13.
20  LNR [Ellen Henrietta Ranyard], *The Missing Link, or Bible-Women in the
    Homes of the London Poor* (New York: Robert Carter & Brothers, 1860), 25.
21  "Mission to the Teloogoos," *Baptist Missionary Magazine*, 1869, vol. 49,
    no. 7, p. 258.

Telugu Biblewomen in the colonial period
Archives of the Evangelical Lutheran Church in America.

indicates their relationship with the local missionaries. Beth-
sheba, the third on the payroll, served in Nandyala. Of the
three, it is highly plausible that Rueben was a Dalit, if Porter's
interpretation of her caste identity is to be trusted, and Beth-
sheba a Reddy.[26]

Missionary reports do not mention the family name or the
caste identity of Lydia. However, the manner of her visits to
the LMS congregation and the resistance of her family to her
conversion hint at her non-Dalit background. Hailing from

22  Martha Porter in *Missing Link Magazine*, April 1871, 125.
23  Martha Porter, "A Hindoo Women's Inquiry—Who Then Will Save
    Me? Who?," *Missing Link Magazine*, February 1872, 51. It is likely that
    the mother and son were related to Peter Wesley, who was employed by
    Edward Porter as an evangelist.
24  *Missing Link Magazine*, September 1871, 276.
25  *Missing Link Magazine*, April 1871, 125. I stand corrected in regard to my
    identification with the Reformed Church in America.
26  *Missing Link Magazine*, March 1877, 86.

Visakhapatnam, Lydia heard of Christianity through a group of native Christian women assembled in a house-church.[27] After visiting them four times, she decided to embrace Christianity and was subsequently baptized in the local LMS chapel in the early 1860s. She eventually moved south to Nellore and worked with American Baptist missionaries. Lydia preferred to live in mission compounds rather than with her non-Christian family, as her association with Christianity would have stigmatized them, and in turn, her family might have attempted to interfere with her Christian practice.[28] Commended by American Baptist missionaries for her "sweetest and most stirring language,"[29] Lydia worked with them for more than thirty years from the early 1860s in various positions.[30] When the office of Biblewoman was imported to the region, women missionaries did not have to look far to find someone more eligible than Lydia.

As the above-mentioned appointments indicate and other recruitment patterns attest, the majority of the Biblewomen were of dominant caste origins. The tides of massive Dalit conversions were only beginning when the office of Biblewoman was imported, and there would not have been many Dalit women considered eligible for the office. Literacy and the ability to visit all neighborhoods—caste and outcaste—were key to doing the job, two things inaccessible to Dalits. With increased access to education and the founding of Bible training schools for women, more Dalit women increasingly joined the profession in the twentieth century and diversified the office.

27  David Downie, *The Lone Star: A History of the Telugu Mission of the American Baptist Foreign Mission Society* (Philadelphia: Judson, 1924), 51.
28  Downie, 53.
29  "The Story of the Teloogoo Mission," *Baptist Missionary Magazine*, 1872, vol. 52, no. 5, p. 178.
30  Downie, *Lone Star*, 53.

The Bible has been at the center of Biblewomen's work. In their interactions with women, they narrated tales from the Bible. Their songs related the gospel story in streets and on verandas. Narrating and singing faith were not novel to Telugu women. Reading and reciting Scriptures were. Equipped to read the Scriptures, a skill denied to them earlier often because of their gender and their social location as Dalits, Biblewomen memorized and recited scriptural texts. In doing so, they challenged the religious scholars in other religious traditions who often were male and Brahmin. For example, Mariamma's previous work experience also helped her candidature. Having been a Dalit (Madiga) priestess, she acquired the skills and confidence to engage in "wordy fights" with Brahmin priests.[31]

The work of Telugu Biblewomen was not confined to preaching. Drawing from their evangelical faith, Biblewomen occasionally extended their services to clinics and schools. As mentioned earlier, Mary Wesley of Proddatur, one of the earliest Biblewomen, hosted a medicine dispensary and served as a Biblewoman-nurse along with her doctor-son. They visited patients at hospitals and dispensaries. For example, Abishekamma—a chief nurse and Biblewoman at Medak Hospital, founded by the Wesleyan Methodist missionaries in 1896—repeatedly related this story to waiting outpatients.[32] Biblewomen carried medications and vaccines to villages in times of plagues and distributed them. Reminiscing the life of Charles W. Posnett, a British Wesleyan missionary in Medak, F. Colyer Sackett records that the villagers during a plague requested a Dalit Biblewoman to transport medicine to

31  Daniel, *Moving with the Times*, 47. The ability to debate with Brahmin men was a celebrated gift. See also Cannaday, "Meenakshi," 83–84.

32  Arley Isabel Munson, *Jungle Days: Being the Experiences of an American Woman Doctor in India* (New York: Appleton, 1913), 43. This Bible story is recorded in Luke 2:1–24.

them.[33] According to him, the local community respected the
Biblewoman for her conveying the medicine at the risk of her
health.[34] Their training in basic hygiene and the Bible prepared
Biblewomen to care for and preach to those in hospitals.

Given their education, Biblewomen occasionally played
the dual roles of preaching in houses and teaching in schools.
Biblewomen, by and large, were literate, having attended training classes and normal schools founded by the missionaries.[35]
For example, upon his arrival in Samarlakota, Americus V.
Timpany, a Canadian Baptist missionary, started a primary
school there in 1880. His only employee, Ellen, an Anglo-
Indian Biblewoman, was its founding teacher.[36] Occasionally, a Biblewoman played all the roles that a school needed.
Neela, a Biblewoman in Bobbili, was a chef, teacher, and
matron of the boarding school. Her colleague and sister-in-
law, G. Sayamma, was a schoolteacher and Biblewoman.[37]

With Bibles in their hands, Biblewomen traversed within
and beyond their neighborhoods. This practice took Biblewomen to houses of Dalit, Muslim, and Hindu women, some
of which were traditionally closed to them. By becoming
female preachers and traveling to other caste neighborhoods,

33  F. Colyer Sackett, *Posnett of Medak* (London: Cargate, 1951), 125.

34  Sackett, 125.

35  *Among the Telugus: Canadian Baptist Foreign Missions Annual Report* (Toronto:
Canadian Baptist Foreign Missionary Society, 1924), 51.

36  Here, Ellen should not be confused with Ellen E. Folsom, an unaffiliated American single-woman missionary located in Kakinada. Folsom
eventually joined ranks with Canadian Baptist missionaries in the region.
The complete name of Ellen is not mentioned, but there is a reference to
her in *Canadian Missionary Link* 3 (1880), 14; Mary J. Frith, "Bible Wom-
en's Work," in *The "Lone Star" Jubilee: Papers and Discussions of the Conference
Held in Nellore, February 5–10, 1886, to Celebrate the Fiftieth Anniversary of the
American Baptist Telugu Mission* (Madras, India: Addison, 1886), 54.

37  Matilda F. Churchill, *Letters from My Home in India*, ed. Grace McLeod
Rogers (Toronto: McClelland, Goodchild & Stewart, 1916), 283.

Biblewomen boldly transgressed the social boundaries of the day that restricted visits beyond one's caste neighborhoods.

There were differences between the practices of zenana workers and Biblewomen, but these variances were negligible. With a few exceptions, zenana workers visited the homes of Muslim and Hindu women and taught reading skills and Bible lessons regularly. Zenana workers mostly were women of dominant caste backgrounds. On the other hand, Biblewomen visited women of all backgrounds and focused on teaching the Bible.[38] Occasionally, Biblewomen served as zenana workers as well.

### Health Workers: Agents of Healing

Caring for health needs had been integral to evangelical piety. The profession of nursing was construed as the second arm to that of Biblewomen, as one cared for the body while the other attended to the soul.[39] After all, the body needs to be cared for "as well as" the soul, as "human souls live in bodies."[40] One's physical and social environments shape their spiritual welfare, and the latter manifests itself in one's health and public life, the British evangelicals believed. As evangelicals, Protestant missionaries recognized the need to care for both. As a result, some of them were trained physicians and nurses. With their emphasis on compassion, Roman Catholics were equally active in ministering to the total needs of the Telugus. Of course, their commitment to Jesus, known for his healings, may have spurred this interest.

---

38  Mary Eleanor A. Chamberlain, *Fifty Years in Foreign Fields: A History of Five Decades of the Women's Board of Foreign Missions, Reformed Church in America* (New York: Board of Foreign Missions of the Reformed Church in America, 1925), 57.

39  LNR [Ellen Henrietta Ranyard], *Nurses for the Needy or Bible-Women Nurses in the Homes of the London Poor* (London: James Nisbet, 1875), vii.

40  LNR, "Our Agents and Their Support," in *Missing Link*, 291.

At their arrival, missionaries established general hospitals as well as special hospitals. In the Northern Circars, John Davis, a Canadian Baptist missionary, founded a leprosy hospital in Ramachandrapuram in 1893.[41] In the state of Hyderabad, Isabel Kerr, a British Wesleyan medical missionary, founded a leprosy hospital in Dichpally in 1911.[42] In the southern region, Thomas V. Campbell, an LMS missionary and an alumnus of the University of Edinburgh, established hospitals in Jammalamadugu and Chikkaballapur as well as the Arogyavaram Tuberculosis Sanatorium in 1915. In the northern end of coastal Andhra, Canadian Baptist missionaries Ben Gullison and Mary Evelyn Gullison founded an eye hospital in Sompeta in 1935.[43]

With more than half of the missionary personnel being women and some of them trained as doctors and nurses, there was an augmented focus on women's health, especially on maternity care. American Reformed missionaries in Rayalaseema started a hospital in Madanapalle in 1863 with a vision to care for women's health. Between 1884 and 1906, Protestant missionaries founded at least thirteen clinics among the Telugus.[44] Data collected from six missionary societies illustrate the missionary enthusiasm to work for the health of the local women. With their emphasis on health, Roman Catholic missionaries were equally active in medical missions.

41 John E. Davis, *The Life Story of a Leper: Autobiography of John E. Davis* (Toronto: CBFMB, 1918), 170.
42 John Pritchard, *Methodists and Their Missionary Societies 1900–1996* (New York: Ashgate, 2014), 95–96.
43 Paul Dekar, *For the Healing of the Nations: Baptist Peacemakers* (Macon, GA: Smyth & Helwys, 1993), 152.
44 These were in Guntur (1884), Dummagudem (1885), Nellore (1891), Hanumakonda (1894), Yelamanchili (1895), Akividu (1895), Chirala (1895), Nalgonda (1896), Medak (1897), Rajahmundry (1899), Srikakulam (1899), Pithapuram (1904), and Vuyyuru (1906).

As part of equipping the local agency, Christian missionaries started nursing schools and medical colleges to train native women. The Vellore Christian Medical College, founded by Ida Scudder, an Indian-born American Reformed missionary, was the most reputed of such in the south. Started as a one-bed hospital for women and children at the turn of the twentieth century, it eventually became the Missionary Medical School for Women in 1914. An ecumenical venture in its inception, the Missionary Medical School for Women trained numerous female doctors for mission hospitals in the southern and the central provinces.[45] Many of its alumnae served in the Telugu regions.

Dhanamma Joshua Chegudi from Guntur was a part of the first batch of graduates to matriculate with a licentiate medical practitioner diploma from the Missionary Medical School for Women. Upon her graduation in 1922, Dhanamma had joined the mission hospital in Guntur founded by Ann Sarah Kugler.[46] Before proceeding to study at the (Vellore) Missionary Medical School for Women, Dhanamma had earlier studied at a mission college in Chennai in 1917.[47] Her father's name, Joshua, suggests that she was raised by Christian parents.[48] Her sister Victoria was a schoolteacher at the local Stall Girls High School, where both sisters studied.[49] After serving at Kugler Women's Hospital for ten years, Dhanamma moved to Repalle and opened a private clinic there, using her medical

45  Maina Chawla Singh has an illuminating chapter on Vellore Christian Medical College in her book *Gender, Religion, and "Heathen Lands": American Missionary Women in South Asia, 1860s–1940s* (New York: Garland, 2000), 281–312.

46  Dhanamma succeeded a Malayalee doctor named Paru.

47  *Lutheran Women's Work*, March 1923, 87; Anna Sarah Kugler, *Guntur Mission Hospital, Guntur, India* (Philadelphia: Women's Missionary Society of the United Lutheran Church in America, 1928), 38.

48  *Lutheran Women's Work*, November 1923, 425.

49  Kugler, *Guntur Mission Hospital*, 38.

skills beyond the mission settings.[50] According to Kugler, the American Lutherans invested in her education, likely with an understanding that she would work for a designated period in one of the mission hospitals.[51]

Matriculating from the Vellore Medical College in 1928, Mary Moses Karra, a licentiate medical practitioner, joined the Lutheran Mission Hospital in Rajahmundry.[52] After serving there at the women's hospital for two years, she moved to and supervised the Augustana Hospital in Bhimavaram, founded in 1931.[53] She moved back to Rajahmundry Mission Hospital in 1935. The missionary chroniclers do not mention the caste identity of Mary Moses, but her family name suggests she was a Dalit. Born in a Christian family to Shanthamma and Moses Karra, Mary Moses may have had access to education in mission schools.[54]

Looking at the family names, it is not hard to suspect that both Doctor Dhanamma Joshua and Doctor Mary Moses were of Dalit background. In an age when educational opportunities for girls were sparse and, if available, limited to girls of dominant caste backgrounds, medical training of Dalit women was unlikely. As cultural centers of Telugu society, Guntur and Rajahmundry had women's schools. Dalit Christian women took advantage of the educational opportunities offered in and

---

50  *The Annual Report of the Foreign Missions of the United Lutheran Church in America* (Baltimore: BFMULCA, 1932), 17. See also Swavely, *One Hundred Years*, 189.

51  Kugler, *Guntur Mission Hospital*, 38.

52  Martin Luther Dolbeer, R. D. Augustus, and Clarence H. Swavely, *Biographical Record of the Pastors, Missionaries and Prominent Laymen of the United Lutheran Church Mission and the Andhra Evangelical Lutheran Church* (Rajahmundry, India: Silver Jubilee Committee of the AELC, 1955), 130.

53  Barbara E. DeRemer, "The Medical Work of the Mission," in Swavely, *One Hundred Years*, 283.

54  Dolbeer, Augustus, and Swavely, *Biographical*, 130.

by the missionary establishment to pursue their basic and professional education.

To support the medical services offered in their hospitals, Christian missionaries established numerous nursing schools long before the establishment of the Missionary Medical School for Women in Vellore. American Lutheran missionaries started nursing schools in Guntur (1899), Rajahmundry (1918), Rentachintala (1921), and Chirala (1924).[55] According to the data available, American Lutheran missionaries trained more than 308 nurses by 1941—that is, seven or eight women every year.[56] Most of their alumnae sought and found employment in mission hospitals.

Given the stigma attached to the profession, Telugu women initially did not show interest in the field but gradually found this to be an attractive employment option.[57] The profession required touching bodies, and there might have been resistance and fears from caste and Dalit women to this critical sector. Declaring a new day in the region, F. P. Manly, an American Lutheran missionary, observed that working in hospitals provided women, most of who were of Dalits, avenues to enter the lives of "aristocratic Hindu homes."[58]

### Schoolteachers: Empowering Education

By the end of the nineteenth century, women had gained access to literacy. The colonial administration of the Madras Presidency, local maharajahs, Hindu reformers, and Christian

---

55  Hilma Levine, "Training School for Nurses," in Swavely, *One Hundred Years*, 287–89.

56  Levine, 289–90. There is no definite data on the number of alumni at Rentachintala Hospital Training Center.

57  Levine, 287.

58  F. P. Manly, "The New Day in India," *Missions: American Baptist International Magazine*, November 1923, 598.

missionaries together facilitated this access.[59] It needs to be located in the contemporaneous cultural reforms in terms of the marriage age of girls and widow marriage. Telugu women engineered and perpetuated the reforms as students and teachers.

In the 1870s, there was a sudden and dramatic upsurge of interest both to start and to attend girls' schools. The number of schools designated for girls attests to this. According to John Greenfield Leonard, a social historian, there were only 136 schools for girls in 1870 in the Madras Presidency, and the number of girls' schools increased fourfold in the next ten years—that is, 546 schools by 1880.[60] Ninety-eight more schools were added in 1881. It may not have been the sole catalyst, but the 1867 visit of Mary Carpenter, a British social activist, had a role in women's education on the subcontinent.[61] Influenced by the ideology of Brahmo Samaj and Western liberal thought, local princes started numerous schools for girls.[62] For example, in 1868, the maharajah of Pithapuram founded a girls' school in Kakinada with monthly and annual grants for its maintenance.[63] In the same year, the maharajah of Vizianagaram founded one for Brahmin and Kshatriya girls in his capital.

---

59 John Greenfield Leonard, *Kandukuri Viresalingam (1848–1919): A Biography of an Indian Social Reformer* (Hyderabad, India: Telugu University Press, 1991), 26; Yallampalli Vaikuntham, *Education and Social Change in South India: Andhra, 1880–1920* (Madras, India: New Era, 1982), 123.

60 Leonard, *Kandukuri*, 26.

61 Ramakrishna, *Social Reform in Andhra*, 93. Vaikuntham provides detailed statistics about the number of schools founded for boys and girls in the 1870s. See Vaikuntham, *Education and Social Change*, 15.

62 Brahmo Samaj was a nineteenth-century movement of reform-minded Hindus who believed in one God and campaigned for women's rights. Founded in 1828 by Raja Ram Mohan Roy, the society sought to reform Hinduism by welcoming ideological resources from other faiths.

63 Ramakrishna, *Social Reform in Andhra*, 93.

Brahmin dissenters—such as Viresalingam Kandukuri and Venkata Apparao Gurajada, architects of the Telugu Renaissance—for their part initiated social reforms within the caste Hindu communities.[64] Influenced by the Brahmo ideology, they advocated widow marriages and boldly solemnized some. They denounced the early marriage of girls. It was not until 1929 that the colonial government, with its Sarada (Sharda) Act, intervened and legislated the minimum age for marriage to be fourteen, and that too after intense lobbying by the All India Women's Conference.[65] While not abandoning the Hindu faith, Telugu "social reformers" reinterpreted the Hindu scriptures to improve women's social status. They used the girls' schools that local princes founded to disseminate their ideas. For example, in 1879, Viresalingam lectured at the Vizianagaram Maharajah's Hindu Girls School, founded by the maharajah, on the practice of widow marriage.[66]

The reforming programs of the Brahmin dissenters and Kshatriyas focused only on the social status of caste women, especially those of Brahmin origins.[67] According to V. Ramakrishna, a social historian, these reform movements offered an alternative to Christianity, which by then was drawing conversions from Dalit communities and was making inroads into the caste communities.[68]

Recognizing the need for women's education and the opportunity to introduce literacy and Christianity, Christian missionaries established schools, some of which were for girls.

---

64 Vakulabharanam Rajagopal, "Fashioning Modernity in Telugu: Viresalingam and His Interventionist Strategy," *Studies in History* 21, no. 1 (2005): 45–77.

65 Rebecca Adami, *Women and the Universal Declaration of Human Rights* (New York: Routledge, 2020), 70.

66 Leonard, *Kandukuri*, 85.

67 Yogendra K. Malik, *South Asian Intellectuals and Social Change: A Study of the Role of Vernacular-Speaking Intelligentsia* (New Delhi, India: Heritage, 1982), 316.

68 Ramakrishna, *Social Reform in Andhra*, 186.

Due to dominant caste parents' resistance to send their children to study with Dalits, some missionaries occasionally made concerted efforts to enlist caste girls by establishing "caste schools." The new generation of literate women these schools had produced eventually became teachers and championed literacy among the women.

The curricula in the mission schools aimed at teaching what they called the three Rs. The skills they wanted to impart were (1) reading, (2) writing, and (3) arithmetic. They also had a subtle fourth R, a less pronounced but consistent program to teach their Christian faith.[69] As an ancient civilization, Telugu culture was not new to letters and numbers, but the knowledge of them had been denied to Dalits. Missionaries had an agenda in introducing the first three. With their version of literacy and calculations, they were ushering Telugus into the Western Enlightenment values of liberty, equality, and comradery, an ethos that would potentially undermine traditional Telugu learning. As people of the book, missionaries wanted to read and grasp the Bible, hoping that the very reading of the text would transform the latter's worldview. After all, building up leadership for the society and church and thereby influencing Telugu society was their agenda.

Denied access to literacy for centuries, Dalits were drawn to mission schools. The dominating groups not only denied Dalits the basic skills of reading and writing but also penalized them for attempting to acquire them. The popular tale of Ekalavya represents the stealthy denial of education to Dalits. According to the story, Ekalavya, a determined Dalit, mastered the art of archery by watching a skilled archer but without the permission of the latter. As customary, the grateful student wanted to pay *gurudakshina* (an honorarium to the teacher). However,

---

69 Drach and Kuder, *Telugu Mission*, 235. See also Hibbert Ware, *Telugu Country*, 141.

offering a gift was risky. As a Dalit, Ekalavya was not permitted to approach the caste "teacher." And he had neither sought nor received permission to learn the art, knowing very well that it would not be granted. Having gathered courage, Ekalavya approached the master archer and offered to give the latter whatever he wished. The disingenuous master stealthily demanded that Ekalavya cut off his thumb and offer it as an honorarium, a move that would ultimately prevent him from using his newly acquired skills. This folklore highlights the outright denial of literacy to Dalits.

The abilities to read and write opened up for Dalits nontraditional employment opportunities and thereby challenged the status quo. In an agrarian society, the economy relied heavily on the labor of Dalits, and they were proficient in farming. Since agriculture provided seasonal opportunities and the wages thereof were meager, often at the mercy of the landlords, Dalits possessed additional sets of competencies. During the year, they herded the cattle, which ensured their daily food and also assured the landlords of their loyalty. Landlords rewarded their labor and loyalty in kind, annually as grains and on the days of herding as food. While at home, men processed leather and produced accessories useful in herding, irrigation, and farming. With processed leather, they also sewed sandals. They wove the hay on the farms into threads, essential at homes and in the farms. Women, on the other hand, wove together baskets (carry bags) out of coconut and toddy leaves. None of these splendid skills required literacy, the key to unlocking the literary wisdom in the Telugu tradition.

The lack of access to the Telugu texts, however, denied Dalits an opportunity to read and reinterpret the texts that legitimized their social status. It also confined them to subordinate occupations that the dominators associated with impurity. The British colonial administration muddied the waters by appointing Dalits in government sectors such as public works, municipalities, judiciaries, and railroads, some of which required some level of literacy. Dalits, seeking to transgress the social boundaries, looked for opportunities to acquire literary skills. Dalit women found allies in those committed to their education.

The dearth of personnel in the mission schools and the need for local agency warranted the missionaries to recruit Telugu schoolteachers—both women and men. There were not many equipped to perform the given tasks—hence the need for teacher training. John Clay, an SPG missionary, started a teacher training school in Mutyalapadu, near Kadapa, as early as 1860.[70] With a heightened focus on the education of girls, missionaries encouraged the Telugu Christian women to become schoolteachers. As a result, almost all denominations started teacher training schools and enrolled women.[71] Writing as late as 1912, after almost three decades of educating women, G. Hibbert Ware, an SPG missionary, named the need for women teachers as their "greatest."[72] Given the agenda of imparting religious education, most of those employed were Christian. The schoolteachers created for themselves opportunities to subtly or openly introduce their evangelical faith and influence children in their classrooms in their formative years.

### Weaving a Narrative: Women Writers

With newly acquired skills in reading and writing, Christian women contributed to social and religious life through short stories, poems, and songs. More than twenty of the sixty Dalit women listed in the Dalit anthology compiled by Gogu Shyamala are identified as Christians or identified with Christian

---

70  Hibbert Ware, *Telugu Country*, 62.
71  American Lutheran missionaries started one in Tarlapudi, Reformed missionaries in Chittoor, and Canadian Baptist missionaries in Kakinada, to name a few.
72  Hibbert Ware, *Telugu Country*, 170.

families or mission schools. As mentioned in the introduction, many Dalits in the postcolonial period chose not to identify themselves as Christians because of the legal implications such a move would have on their employment. The federal and state governments do not employ—or, if already employed, penalize—them under their protective discrimination provisions. Among others, these Dalit Christian women constantly challenge the caste and gender injustices in Telugu culture.

Songs by at least five women feature in the Telugu Christian hymnal (*Andhra Kraistava Kirtanalu*). The ratio of ninety-five male bards compared to five female hymnists may not speak highly of the space women find in the hymnal. However, all five songwriters were of Dalit descent, attesting to the levels of education women in Dalit communities have reached. Two of the five were schoolteachers. Songs by women consistently celebrate the life of Jesus, and when focused on daily living, they are centered on the Christian family. They drew extensively from the Bible.[73]

Born in Dachepalle in 1890, Gnanaratnamma Philip studied at Stall Girls High School in Guntur. She had eventually taught at her alma mater.[74] Of the seven hymns she composed, two of them were meant to be sung at the beginning of worship. Her hymn "Chakkani Yesuswami Na Chakki Kegudhinche" (Beloved Jesus has drawn close to me) is noteworthy for our purposes. While emphasizing the divine immanence, Gnanaratnamma extolls God's care for every individual. "The one who sends sun and rain on the trees also endows me with joys and sorrows," she claims.[75] Later in the hymn, she prays that the Lord will grant her the hands of Martha and the mind of Mary, recognizing the importance of both in the Christian

---

73  Gogu Syamala, *Nalla Proddhu: Dalita Streela Sahityam* [Black dawn: Dalit women's literature] (Hyderabad, India: Hyderabad Book Trust, 2003), 39–41, 48–50.

74  Rayi, *Telugulo Chraistava Sahityam*, 338–39; Syamala, *Nalla Proddhu*, 38–39.

75  Syamala, *Nalla Proddhu*, 39.

faith.[76] The songs of praise do not present themselves to be departures from the songs her male counterparts composed, but the accent on the divine imminence and affirmation of Martha and Mary as models of Christian piety do.

Krupa Kommu's hymn "Sri Yesundu Janminche Reyilo Nedu" (Lord Jesus is born tonight) is a popular song composed in folk music and sung enthusiastically with dance annually during the Advent season both in sanctuaries and in streets. In this, Krupa highlights the humble origins of Jesus Christ and seamlessly helps the singer imagine Jesus as one among the Dalits. As hinted earlier, the hymns by Gulbanamma Vesapogu (1905–71; who was a headmistress of the Preston Institute in Jangaon), Chandhramma Katta, and Vijaya Pilli highlight the themes of a Christian home and character.[77] Thus, due to the literacy acquired, these Dalit women have through hymns contributed to the Telugu Christian thought and piety.

### Significance

What have these professions done to the women? Most of the women on the mission payroll—Biblewomen, health workers, and schoolteachers—were Dalits. Along with their men, Dalit women traditionally were breadwinners. They toiled in the agricultural lands, sowing and reaping. While at home, they wove baskets, umbrellas, and fans. They contributed to the local economy as much as their men did. Their earnings fed their families. Women's economic contributions to their families and villages did not guarantee them an equal share in

---

76  Rayi, *Telugulo Chraistava Sahityam*, 340; Syamala, *Nalla Proddhu*, 39.

77  William Arthur Stanton, *Out of the East: India's Search for God* (New York: Fleming H. Revell, 1938), 72; Syamala, *Nalla Proddhu*, 40; Rayi, *Telugulo Chraistava Sahityam*, 343.

decision-making because of the way their labor was compensated. The landlords compensated women in kind, mostly in grains and clothing during the harvesting seasons. The income earned was a family wage, as Dalit families worked for the families of the landlords, whereas the wages earned in cash as Biblewomen, health workers, and schoolteachers offered women opportunities to plan their spending. The wages they received may not have been comparable to those of men, but they still earned a modicum of bargaining power.

What have these professional women done to the Christian community? With the opportunities these professions offered, women could and did impact the evolution of Telugu Christianity. As mentioned earlier, Biblewomen visited homes and introduced the Christian faith. New converts and nascent congregations looked up to them for instruction in seasons of life when religion mattered. Biblewomen offered advice in matters of faith and practice. Meanwhile, doctors and nurses demonstrated the Christian values and occasionally introduced their faith to patients and families when opportunities arose. Meetings with patients invariably opened up conversations about beliefs. Schoolteachers, on the other hand, modeled and occasionally taught the evangelical lifestyle. Through their lives and work, these professional women transmitted and translated the Christian message, much beyond the pulpit. Together, they have inspired generations of girls to seek education and pursue careers beyond their homes and agricultural fields.

What have these women leaders done to the Christian message? Of course, the context of interpretation determined their rendering of the text. Most of the available topics point to women's fascination with the Gospel stories. According to an antecedent reported by Arley Isabel Munson, Abishekamma, a chief nurse and Biblewoman at Medak Hospital, repeatedly told the story of Elizabeth's conception, one of the Lukan infancy narratives.[78] The story would certainly have appealed to this audience and heightened their hopes for children, as most of them were childless and were visiting the hospital because they wanted children.[79]

If missionary reports are any indication, according to John Carman, an American Baptist missionary, Biblewomen centered their teachings on the life and ministry of Jesus Christ.[80] They highlighted the texts in the Gospels where Jesus interacted with women and children.[81] The importance afforded to children and women by God would have drawn women toward their message. Jesus was not merely a teacher or preacher, according to them. He was a healer, one who cared for their infirmities.

The political dynamics of the colonial context and the missionaries' presence, no doubt, influenced the reception and articulation of the Christian faith by the local Christians. So did their social aspirations, political interests, and willingness to accommodate one another. The confluences among Hindu traditions, Christian beliefs, and Dalit worldviews continued in the postcolonial context but in a new environment and with heightened confidence among the Telugu Christians. The God they preached cared for the immediate needs of the people.

---

78  Munson, *Jungle Days*, 43. This Bible story is recorded in Luke 2:1–24.

79  Munson, 43.

80  John Spencer Carman, *Rats, Plague, and Religion: Stories of Medical Mission Work in India* (Philadelphia: Judson, 1936), 223.

81  Carman, 229.

# Part II

# 5

# The Spirit at the Edges
## *Telugu Pentecostals*

Pentecostalism among the Telugus emerged at the margins of an already marginalized Christian community in the 1930s. It grew out of those Dalit Christians neglected in the liturgical churches and longing for the freedom of worship as well as of the Sudhra Christians who were reluctant to associate with churches dominated by Dalit Christians. Disenchanted self-made Dalit preachers appropriated the Pentecostal beliefs and missionized among the caste communities. With its countercultural practices, the movement drew from and challenged the dominant cultures within the liturgical churches as well as those in Telugu society. The movement provided a relatively higher space for women to exercise their gifts of leadership. The eventual takeover by the Sudhra leadership in the 1960s or the Dalit preachers' emulation of the same resulted in the Sanskritization of Telugu Pentecostalism even while cementing its global networks. This chapter narrates the story of Telugu Pentecostalism and highlights its journey from being a countercultural movement toward Sanskritization.

### Setting the Tone

Two important watershed periods shed light on the following three chapters: the identity politics of the 1930s and the formation of states on a linguistic basis. In the 1930s, the massive conversion among the Dalits was at its peak but was beginning to be challenged. The ideological struggle between two politicians dominated the national conversations on freedom. Recognizing the simmering nationalist anger and the need to share power with the locals, the British crown constituted provincial assemblies and conducted elections. In 1933, Mohandas Gandhi, a Gujarati Baniya, fasted unto death to deny Dalits representation in legislative bodies. Seeking to create the myth of one nation without distinct interests, he was critical of Dalit conversions to Christianity, as conversions would attest to and reinforce multiple interest groups on the subcontinent. Gandhi was equally hostile toward Christian missionaries not for their civil contributions but for becoming allies to Dalits in religious conversions. In the process, Gandhi asked the Christian missionaries to abstain from proselytization.

Under the pretext of providing dignity, which was the need of the hour, Gandhi constituted Harijan Sevak Sangh, a group of self-appointed guardians of the Dalits. The group organized a cleanliness drive in the Dalit hamlets, as if Dalits, who cleaned the villages, needed to be "clean." They also provided alternative educational opportunities. Between 1932 and 1934, Harijan Sevak Sangh ran forty-one evening schools, eleven day schools, and nineteen hostels to wean Dalits from mission schools.[1] Meanwhile, Suddhi Sangams, related and parallel groups, ordered the Dalit Christians to renounce their Christian identity.[2]

On the other side of the conversation was Bhimrao Ramji Ambedkar, a Marathi Dalit leader, highlighted the distinct interest groups on the subcontinent and demanded that each should be represented in the legislative assemblies. He recognized the

---

1  Yagati, *Dalits' Struggle for Identity*, 87.
2  Swavely, *One Hundred Years*, 30.

civil utility of religion and viewed religious conversion as a political weapon.[3] In 1935, he declared his interest to embrace an alternative religion that assured social equality and dignity to its adherents. Reverberations of the debate were felt among the Telugus.

Meanwhile, recognizing the impact of religious conversions on social status and mobility, Sudhras, a substrate of society considered higher than Dalits, showed interest in Christianity.[4] Many missionary reports hint at a heightened interest among Sudhras in Christianity, so much so that the Sudhra conversions elicited a debate beyond the local level. Frank Whittaker, a British Wesleyan missionary, wrote an essay in the *National Council of Churches Review* about this emerging phenomenon.[5] W. J. T. Small reports about a "caste" movement in Telangana, while Martin Luther Dolbeer discusses one in coastal Andhra.[6] In his study commissioned by the council, Jarrell W. Pickett, argues that these conversions were due to the social mobility and personal lifestyles the Sudhras observed in Dalit Christians.[7] According to Geoffrey Oddie, a social historian, Sudhra Christians constituted at least 10 percent of the Christians in and around Vijayawada.[8] The Anglican diocese at Dornakal welcomed more than seven thousand Sudhra converts by 1931.[9] Given the caste hostilities and the

---

3 Viswanathan, *Outside the Fold*, 213–14.

4 Pickett, *Christian Mass Movements*, 125.

5 Frank Whittaker, "The Caste Movement towards Christianity in Northern Hyderabad," *NCCR* 53, no. 10 (October 1933): 517–31.

6 W. J. T. Small, "The 'Caste' Movement in Hyderabad," *NCCR* 51, no. 2 (February 1931): 79–84; Martin Luther Dolbeer, "The Caste Mass Movement in the Telugu Area," *NCCR* 53, no. 8 (August 1933): 420–29.

7 Pickett, *Christian Mass Movements*, 299.

8 Geoffrey Oddie, ed., *Religion in South Asia: Religious Conversion and Revival Movements in South Asia in Medieval and Modern Times* (London: Curzon, 1977), 80.

9 Oddie, 76.

stigma attached to associating with Dalits, Sudhra converts
may have resulted in Sudhras' quests for alternative avenues
and forms of being a Christian, which we will analyze in the
next three chapters.

What, then, was happening in the mid-nineteenth century?
Weakened after World War II, encouraged at the prospect of a
well-drafted constitution, and helpless after a relentless struggle
for freedom led by the Indian National Congress, the British
left the subcontinent in 1947, resulting in the birth of modern

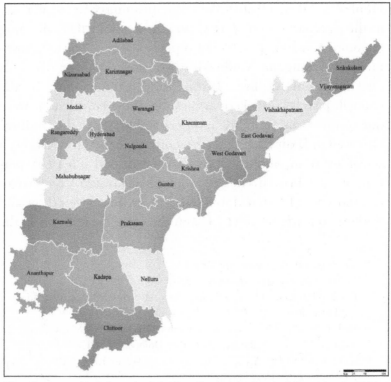

The district map of the united Andhra Pradesh before its bifurcation in 2014
C. Dev, "Andhra Pradesh Districts Map," Wikimedia Commons, September 14,
2008, https://commons.wikimedia.org/wiki/File:Andhra_Pradesh_districts
_map.svg.

India. The Indian Union occupied the state of Hyderabad in 1948. After nearly a decade of negotiations, the state of Andhra Pradesh was formed in 1956, with districts where Telugu was the primary language. Christian missionaries had not left as quickly and suddenly as the British colonial administrators had, but the environment and infrastructure they were accustomed to had dramatically changed. Local leaders grew more vocal and clearer about what they wanted their church to be in the postcolonial period.

### Beginnings of Pentecostalism in India

Citing a lecture he delivered at the Oxford Centre for Mission Studies in 2004, Alan Anderson in his 2013 publication identifies the scattered origins of Pentecostalism on the Indian subcontinent.[10] He traces the eventual emergence of Indian Pentecostalism to the proto-Pentecostal revival movements of the late nineteenth and early twentieth centuries. These precursors were Indigenous in the sense that they were pioneered by natives, but they were not completely local, as they were associated with and had received their impetus from revivalism overseas.

It has multiple forerunners outside the Telugu region. According to Anderson, John Christian Arulappan (1810–67) in Tirunelveli, south of Andhra Pradesh, was the earliest precursor to Pentecostalism. Basing his conclusions on a diary purportedly written by Arulappan and compiled by G. H. Lang, a Brethren writer, as well as reports from contemporary missionaries, Anderson skillfully reconstructs Arulappan's revival movement. A rebel during his theological formation at a CMS training center in Tirunelveli, Arulappan met Brethren missionary Anthony Norris Groves in the early 1830s. Learning

---

10  Allan Anderson, *To the Ends of the Earth: Pentecostalism and the Transformation of World Christianity* (New York: Oxford University Press, 2013), 20.

from Groves the concepts of financial autonomy and separation from the world, Arulappan founded a Christian village.
Due to his concerted evangelistic efforts, Arulappan's movement grew rapidly and spread to thirty villages in three decades.
Like other pietistic mission practices of the day, a Christian
*peta*, a self-sufficient agricultural colony, had a boarding school,
a printing press, a church, and a mission campus. Preachers
were trained to evangelize in adjacent villages. The practices
of speaking in tongues, prophesying, seeing visions, sobbing,
screaming, and falling during prayer continued in the later
Pentecostal movements.[11]

The beginning of the twentieth century witnessed the phe-
nomena of glossolalia and ecstatic baptism in the Spirit in Maha-
rashtra and Mizoram as well. A series of revivals swept through
the Mukti Mission in Pune, north of Telangana, between 1906
and 1907.[12] Aware of the revivals in Wales, Minnie Abrams,
an American Methodist Episcopal missionary assisting Pandita
Ramabai (1858–1922), formed a prayer circle at Mukti Mission
to precipitate revivals in 1905. Both Ramabai and Abrams had
exposure to and connections with the revivals elsewhere in the
world. Ramabai attended the Keswick Convention in 1898,
while her daughter, Manorama, and Abrams witnessed first-
hand the revivals under the leadership of Reuben A. Torrey in
1904 in Australia. The Mukti revivals had a far-reaching impact
globally, Anderson argues. The visitors from Azusa Street and
Abrams's friend May Louise Hoover in Chile bridged the link
between Indigenous revivals and the transnational Pentecostal
movement. The Mukti Mission encouraged the practices of

---

11 Anderson, 24.
12 Anderson, 25–33; Michael Bergunder, *The South Indian Pentecostal Movement
in the Twentieth Century*, Studies in the History of Christian Missions Series
(Grand Rapids, MI: Eerdmans, 2008), 23.

loud crying, unprovoked laughing, trembling, and dancing, at least during the initial period.[13]

Now let us look at the region under study. Parallel revivals swept through the Telugu-speaking regions in the Northern Circars where Baptist missionaries were at work. In Nellore, American Baptist missionaries organized daily prayers for a Madiga congregation specifically to induce revivals. As anticipated, revivals visited the congregation with a "rumbling noise like distant thunder and a simultaneous agonizing cry" in 1906.[14] David Downie, an American Baptist missionary, reports that there was "sobbing" and "crying" in the room.[15] Meanwhile, encouraged by Canadian Baptist missionaries, Telugu Baptists awaited and experienced revivals in and around Akividu in the Krishna district.[16]

A flurry of alignments between local Pentecostals and their American counterparts at the dawn of the twentieth century had direct repercussions in the Northern Circars. To spread the Pentecostal message, preachers from the Azusa Street revivals arrived in India. They found allies among the Protestant missionaries already at work in the region. They collaborated with Indigenous sympathizers. For example, George E. Berg, a former Brethren missionary and the secretary at the Azusa Street church, arrived in Bangalore in 1908.[17] Berg's contacts with former missionary colleagues plus his knowledge of the local cultures proved to be vital links between emerging Pentecostalism in southern India and the classical Pentecostal movement in Azusa Street.

13 Anderson, *To the Ends of the Earth*, 27.
14 David Downie, *From the Mill to Mission Field: An Autobiography of David Downie* (Philadelphia: Judson, 1928), 50.
15 Downie, 50.
16 Craig, *Among the Telugus*, 253.
17 Bergunder, *South Indian Pentecostal Movement*, 24.

For example, Berg collaborated with Robert F. Cook, an Assemblies of God (AG) missionary who arrived in 1913.[18] Together, they joined K. E. Abraham, a Syrian Christian from Kerala, resulting in the birth of the Indian Pentecostal Church of God (IPC) in 1935.[19] The eventual conflict between Abraham and Cook and the latter's meeting with John H. Ingram in 1936 resulted in the formation of the Church of God in India (COG). Subsequently, Cook left the AG in favor of the Church of God. More than sixty IPC congregations, most of which were Dalit, together with Cook affiliated with the COG.[20] Varghese V. Thomas, a Pentecostal historian, interprets this separation as having ensued from a caste-based conflict between Dalit Pentecostals and their Syrian leaders.[21] Mathew Samuel Plathaneth (P. M. Samuel) was a prominent leader in the IPC. Invited by Peter Gurupadam Thullimalli, a Telugu Pentecostal preacher, Samuel visited the Northern Circars and preached in 1932.[22] Gurupadam was instrumental in registering the IPC in Eluru three years later.

---

18  Bergunder, 25.

19  A lot has been written about this alliance. For a more detailed narration and interpretation, please read the following: Varghese V. Thomas, *Dalit Pentecostalism: Spirituality of the Empowered Poor* (Bangalore, India: Asian Trading Corporation, 2008); Bergunder, *South Indian Pentecostal Movement*, 25–32; and Yabbeju (Jabez) Rapaka, *Dalit Pentecostalism: A Study of the Indian Pentecostal Church of God, 1932–2000* (Lexington, KY: Asbury Theological Seminary, 2013), 41–45.

20  Bill George, *Until All Have Heard* (Cleveland, TN: Church of God World Missions, 2010), 413. A Pentecostal congregation from Hyderabad also joined the Church of God. This congregation had been founded by Arthur H. Conney. George provides no further information about this congregation.

21  Thomas, *Dalit Pentecostalism*.

22  Rapaka, *Dalit Pentecostalism*, 64.

## Origins among the Telugus

An invitation from Gurupadam to Samuel attests to the existing Pentecostal presence among the Telugus. Who, then,
introduced Pentecostalism in the region? The origins of Pentecostalism among Telugus can probably be traced back to
Jeevaratnam Lam.[23] Jeevaratnam, a Lutheran minister's son,
attended the United Lutheran Boarding School in Guntur.[24]
He impressed his peers with his artistic skills and with their
help migrated to England, where he earned his livelihood
as a painter. While living in Leeds, England, Jeevaratnam
embraced Pentecostalism in 1926 and, after a two-year ministerial training, returned home with his newfound faith.[25] Upon
returning home, Jeevaratnam organized a Pentecostal congregation in Gudivada. He also founded a children's home and a
high school. He traversed the Northern Circars and preached
until he died in 1960.

More than anything else, Jeevaratnam's skills in healing
ailments and exorcising demons drew converts to Pentecostal
beliefs. Using these extraordinary gifts, Jeevaratnam, a Mala,
reached Dalits and dominant caste Hindus alike. His influence on
two notable church leaders left an indelible impact on Telugu
Christianity. Gurupadam, who invited the IPC missionaries to
the region, heard of the Spirit Baptism through Jeevaratnam.

---

23  Bergunder, *South Indian Pentecostal Movement*; Anderson, *To the Ends of the
    Earth*; Rapaka, *Dalit Pentecostalism*; Pulidindi, *The New Wine-Skins: The Story
    of the Indigenous Missions in Coastal Andhra Pradesh, India* (Delhi: ISPCK,
    2003), 11.
24  Esther B. Harvey, "A Famous Entertainer Becomes a Faith Missionary,"
    *Pentecostal Evangel*, vol. 1063, August 25, 1934, 1.
25  J. H. Boyce, "Indian Christian Convention," *Pentecostal Evangel*, June 9,
    1934, 10. See also Louis F. Boes, "Miracles Wrought thru an Indian
    Sadhu," *Latter Rain Evangel* 26, no. 2 (November 1934): 21.

Gurupadam's sister-in-law Neelam Sundaramma was restored to health when Jeevaratnam prayed for her.[26]

As mentioned earlier, revivalism was not completely new to the Telugu Protestant churches, but the belief in the outpouring of the Holy Spirit was. Jeevaratnam promoted the notion that the Holy Spirit grants healing to individuals without the mediation of physicians and medicine. In the wake of increasing Sudhra interest in Christianity and their reluctance to join Dalit churches, Jeevaratnam offered an alternative within Christianity.

With his enthusiasm to spread the new faith, Gurupadam invited the IPC missionaries to the Northern Circars. Jeevaratnam and Gurupadam were of the Mala community. While the former grew up as a Lutheran, the latter attended a CMS congregation in Machilipatnam. As mentioned in the second chapter, the CMS missionaries Robert T. Noble and Henry W. Fox founded a congregation in Machilipatnam in the 1840s. Educated at Noble High School in Machilipatnam and Andhra Christian College in Guntur, Gurupadam worked in the telegraph department.

Convinced by the Pentecostal teachings and impressed by Jeevaratnam's miraculous powers, Gurupadam started preaching the Pentecostal beliefs to his community in the 1920s. He organized a congregation in Machilipatnam and hosted annual conventions, a practice among Tamil and Malayalee Pentecostals. He had himself attended such conventions, huge gatherings of Pentecostals, in other provinces. It was at one such gathering that Gurupadam met Samuel and invited him to preach among the Telugus. Samuel enthusiastically obliged this request in 1932.

What does the ministry of Gurupadam mean to Pentecostalism? First, Gurupadam inherited the evangelistic enthusiasm

---

26  Rapaka, *Dalit Pentecostalism*, 58.

of Jeevaratnam and transmitted it to the succeeding generations. Second, Gurupadam was not a loner like his older contemporary was. He networked with Tamil and Malayalee Pentecostals. He used these connections to spread the Pentecostal message in the Krishna and the Godavari districts. Dalit Christians had earlier formed alliances with Western missionaries. Third, Gurupadam introduced the practice of holding annual conventions for Telugu Christians as an evangelistic and pedagogical strategy. Most Pentecostal congregations continue the tradition. Many other Protestant churches gradually appropriated the practice. For example, the Andhra Christian Council organized the annual *mahasabhas*.[27] Fourth, Gurupadam and Jeevaratnam initiated the practice of finding mates within the Pentecostal community. Jeevaratnam gave his son Rabel to Gurupadam's daughter Victoria. Many Pentecostals still practice this ecclesial endogamy, lest their children are yoked with mates whose beliefs are different from theirs. Fifth, by inviting Samuel, Gurupadam opened the floodgate of Malayalee missionaries to the Telugu provinces.

### The Spread of Pentecostalism among Telugus

The history of Telugu Pentecostalism can broadly be divided into three periods. The inconvenient but enthusiastic alliance between Malayalee missionaries and Telugu pastors characterizes the first twenty-five years. Malayalee preachers stationed in the Northern Circars trained Telugu pastors, placed them in mission situations, and occasionally paid a modest honorarium. The period between 1960 and 1980 marked a heightened assertion among the Telugu pastors, resulting in the emergence of new Pentecostal denominations. Numerous new Pentecostal churches emerged in the early 1980s. They adapted many indigenous cultural customs that the classical Pentecostals condemned.

### Inconvenient Coalition: 1935–60

Among Dalit Christians, there may have been simmering discontent for missionary association with colonialism, alien liturgical practices, uneasy relationships with missionaries, and the class system among the Dalits between those who benefited from the educational and leadership opportunities offered by the missionaries and those who could not. The Dalit founders of the traditions we will discuss in chapters 6 and 7 seemed to have experienced some of these challenges within the church.

How did Pentecostalism arrive among the Telugus? No single event or individual can be credited for the origin of the tradition. As mentioned earlier, Jeevaratnam imported Pentecostalism from England, and Gurupadam transmitted it. Lazarus Paramjyothi Pachigalla (P. L. Paramjyothi) networked with Pentecostals from elsewhere both to spread the Pentecostal faith and to nuance its local texture.

Paramjyothi was a contemporary of Jeevaratnam and Gurupadam. Like them, he was from the Krishna district. A Madiga from Vuyyuru, Paramjyothi grew up in a Baptist minister's family and attended Canadian Baptist mission schools.[28] He must have heard about Pentecostalism from a visiting Tamil preacher, M. Murugesan. According to an autobiography that his daughter Rachel Jyothi Komanapalli translated into English, Paramjyothi received a divine vision in 1933 at the age of twelve.[29]

---

28 Rapaka, *Dalit Pentecostalism*, 70.
29 Rachel Jyothi Komanapalli, *A Man Sent from God: Life Story and Messages of Apostle P. L. Paramjyoti* (Hyderabad, India: Manna Ministries, 2012), 15.

Pursuing school at McLaurin High School, Paramjyothi attended one year of seminary education, a requisite for
students. At the Baptist Theological Seminary in Kakinada,
Principal John N. McLaurin, a Baptist missionary, encouraged his students to pray for ecstatic experiences.[30] During
high school, Paramjyothi came into contact with P. M. Samuel, who by then had already visited Andhra. After the completion of high school, Paramjyothi became the Baptist pastor
in Vuyyuru, succeeding his father. Paramjyothi introduced
Pentecostal beliefs to his Baptist coreligionists and eventually
organized a Pentecostal congregation in Antarvedipalem four
years later.[31]

Like Gurupadam, Paramjyothi established connections
with Pentecostals from other provinces. He worked closely with
Samuel from 1937 until the latter died in 1981. When they
met, Samuel was an itinerant preacher. Paramjyothi traveled
with Samuel and often translated his non-Telugu colleagues'
sermons at public meetings, ensuring that the Pentecostalism
emerging in the region was ideologically connected to its corol-
laries elsewhere.

Prominent among the guild of Bible teachers, Paramjyothi
trained most of the Telugu Pentecostal preachers during the
first phase. He, along with Samuel, founded the Zion Bible
School, the breeding ground of the IPC, in 1940 and hosted
it in Antarvedipalem for five years.[32] The seminary initially
was held annually for a month or two. It became a mobile
Bible school from 1945 until it was permanently placed in
Gunadala fifteen years later, where Samuel resided.[33] Param-

---

30  Komanapalli, 17. John N. McLaurin was the son of John McLaurin, one
    of the founding missionaries.
31  Bergunder, *South Indian Pentecostal Movement*, 36.
32  Rapaka, *Dalit Pentecostalism*, 72.
33  Bergunder, *South Indian Pentecostal Movement*, 92.

jyothi continued to teach at the seminary even after it moved to Gunadala.

A respected preacher and prolific writer, Paramjyothi was a skilled troubleshooter. As you will read later, he was instrumental in resolving the succession battles when Samuel died in 1981. At both state and national levels, he held important positions, especially after Samuel's death. The IPC elected him as its vice president in 1984, a position he held for three years. Paramjyothi became its acting president in 1987 and served as its president from 1989 until he died in 1996.[34] These positions reveal more of the respect Paramjyothi earned with his experience and faithfulness than the executive power he wielded in the organization. Even while retaining membership and respect within the IPC, he dexterously allied with its rival denomination, World Missionary Evangelism (WME).

Samuel, a Malayalee pastor, deserves a special mention, as he was the face of Pentecostalism for five decades among both local pastors and foreign donors. With his organizational skills and charismatic preaching, Samuel established the IPC and helped its rapid growth in Andhra and Telangana. Born a Marthomite in Kerala, Samuel became a Pentecostal in 1929.[35] Invited to preach in Machilipatnam in 1932, Samuel visited the Northern Circars and eventually moved to Gunadala, near Vijayawada, in 1940.[36] Located there, he traveled across the Telugu territory and introduced Pentecostal beliefs.

Although Samuel was from another region, Telugu Pentecostals embraced him and accepted his leadership. There

34 Rapaka, *Dalit Pentecostalism*, 72.
35 The Marthoma Church is an ecclesiastical body that claims its lineage to the first century. It experienced theological transformation during the eighteenth century due to its encounter with evangelicalism.
36 Bergunder, *South Indian Pentecostal Movement*, 92.

might be multiple reasons for this deference. First, compared
to other pioneers, Samuel was older. He was eighteen years
older than Paramjyothi. In a culture where age earns deference, Samuel received respect even without demanding it.
Second, Telugus often show special respect for guests. Per
the Telugu wisdom, guests are like gods (*athidhi devo bhava*)
and should be treated with reverence. Third, Samuel's caste
identity proved to be an additional source of respect. Samuel
belonged to a Syrian community in Kerala that often claimed
respect on par with the Brahmins in Telugu society. Finding
themselves marginalized both by caste Hindus and by Dalits of the Protestant background, Telugu Pentecostal leaders
would have found Samuel a power center accessible to them.
Fourth, Samuel served as the interlocutor between local pastors and their Western donors. He raised funds for the churches
and controlled finances. Samuel distributed the funds at his
pleasure. He rewarded respect and faithfulness with additional
funds. Having abandoned their traditional sources of income
and famished by economic crunch, Dalit found a patron in
Samuel.

Affiliating with Samuel, Malayalee missionaries and Telugu
preachers established their "own" congregations. They earned
their livelihoods from the offertory plates. The occasional and
limited financial support from the denominational headquarters was usually designated for either church construction or
benevolent projects. In turn, pastors, along with their congregations, attended annual state conventions and contributed
toward their expenses. Pastors also invited denominational
leaders to their local conventions and remunerated them.
Invoking the ancient practice of tithing from Hebrew Scripture,
denominational leaders expected pastors to pay 10 percent of
their income, just as pastors demanded that their congregation
members tithe. Thus financial aid paralleled ideological guidance, and monetary commitments glued local congregations to

the central office in Vijayawada. The real estate that Samuel partially or fully contributed became the property of the IPC, further demanding the loyalty of the pastors to Samuel.

With Samuel arrived many Malayalam missionaries. They settled in urban areas and founded congregations. For example, P. T. Chacko founded a congregation in Eluru before moving to Hyderabad in 1941. He established a few more congregations there. With direct funding from Kerala and abroad, Chacko did not have to depend on Samuel as much as Telugu pastors did.

Following the circuit model of the Methodists, the IPC grouped its congregations into clusters called "areas" for mutual encouragement and edification of pastors. Samuel appointed experienced and loyal area pastors to function as liaisons between him and local pastors. Peter Devasahayam Kanumala of Eluru, Sudharshanam Chatla of Rajanagaram, Rajaratnam Puru-shotham Gaddam of Jedcharla, Ramiah David Kalyanapu of Rajahmundry, and Sudharshanam Joseph Komanapalli of Pala-kollu were the earliest area pastors. These area pastors organized monthly meetings for pastors in their jurisdictions and provided supervision. Their role in the central administration was nominal. The COG has its variant of this hierarchy, with district pastors instead of area pastors. Although administrative structures varied, neither congregations nor local pastors nor area pastors had a role in the decision-making of their denominations.

The IPC monopoly of the "full gospel" was soon challenged by the establishment of the COG in the mid-1950s.[37] Sent by the Church of God World Missions, Harold Turner and his wife, Lucille Turner, arrived in India in 1954.[38] K. G. Phillip registered the society in Kadapa in 1940, but the church did not find its roots in the region until later. The Turners moved

---

37  The COG of the Andhra Pradesh administration declined to provide any
    data regarding its history.
38  George, *Until All Have Heard*, 415. The COG is affiliated with the Church
    of God located in Cleveland, Tennessee.

to Kakinada in 1963.[39] Telugu pastors in the COG faithfully reported to the Turners during this period.

Thus spiritual freedom did not always result in the economic autonomy that the thrice marginalized Telugu pastors would have hoped for in their conversion to Pentecostalism. Because of their social location, caste Hindus did not respect Pentecostal pastors of Dalit descent. Mala and Madiga Christians looked at Pentecostal pastors with contempt because of their faith. Given their economic dependence, Pentecostal pastors had to submit to their spirit-filled Malayalee or American masters.

### Holy Assertions: 1961–81

The second half of the twentieth century was a period of language-based assertions. As mentioned at the beginning of the chapter, Telugus wanted a separate state merely based on the language and developed a sense of Telugu nationalism. It had its ramifications within the Pentecostal church, where Telugu pastors, independent in their territories but yet dependent on their denominational headquarters, looked for opportunities to bypass their Malayalee leaders. Dollars from Dallas literally and symbolically offered such opportunities.

Through his funding and empowering stories, John E. Douglas Sr., a businessman from West Virginia, offered an alternative by founding WME in Dallas, Texas, and funding child development projects among the Telugus. Initially, it was at Samuel's invitation that Douglas visited India in 1957 and invested in the IPC.[40] Douglas was eager to fund the benevolent activities, especially among children, of Telugu pastors. He

---

39  Bergunder, *South Indian Pentecostal Movement*, 99.
40  An email communication from the WME office in Dallas, Texas, dated November 4, 2015. Cf. *Gospel Illuminator* 36, no. 7 (July 1976): 17.

funded some projects through Samuel as well as others directly. Douglas officially registered WME in Dallas, Texas, in 1958 and eleven years later in India. When asked for accountability, Samuel resented Douglas's lack of faith in him, resulting in the rift within the IPC and the birth of WME in India. Samuel resisted Douglas's interference or intervention, citing his belief in "faith mission."[41] By shifting their allegiance to Douglas and receiving unmediated aid, Telugu pastors covertly challenged Samuel's authority even while remaining within the IPC. This did not auger well with Samuel.

What did dollars from Dallas do? (1) Many left the IPC in favor of newer Pentecostal denominations. (2) Some remained with Samuel and were rewarded for their "faithfulness" with increased financial help. (3) A few remained loyal to Samuel and directed the funds from overseas to their families and friends.

First, Ramiah David Kalyanapu (1917–92), a Madiga from Tangutur of the Nalgonda district, was one of the several who abandoned their affiliation with the IPC in favor of WME. A Baptist by birth, David heard about Pentecostalism from Samuel and Paramjyothi in 1938. He joined the IPC congregation in his hometown, Warangal. Spurred by missionary enthusiasm, David resigned his job with the local municipal corporation in 1942 and enrolled in Zion Bible School.[42] After a brief period of ministry in Warangal, David was transferred to Rajahmundry in 1945, from where he served as an area pastor and Bible teacher at Zion Bible School. He also was an editor of *Suvartha Prakashini*, a monthly magazine of the IPC for two decades.[43]

It was while serving with the IPC that David became acquainted with Douglas. Like many of his colleagues, David received occasional funding from Douglas after 1960 for his

---

41  Bergunder, *South Indian Pentecostal Movement*, 96.

42  A telephone interview with Kalyanapu Joseph on October 10, 2015.

43  Pulidindi, *New Wine-Skins*, 50.

charitable institutions, a gesture that provoked Samuel's wrath. David had to choose between the IPC and WME. While the former owned the property where he was living and ministering, the other provided the funding for their much-needed maintenance. David abandoned the IPC in favor of WME. However, David continued to visit the IPC congregations even after leaving the denominations—of course, at the invitations of the local pastors whom he trained. Infuriated by his continued association with the IPC pastors, Samuel eventually prohibited David's ministries within the IPC in 1974.[44] After a protracted legal battle, David retained the properties and served in Rajahmundry with WME until he died in 1992.

Others found avenues of autonomy elsewhere. For example, Gershon Paul Kundeti challenged Samuel's dependence on foreign funds. Accusing Samuel of violating the principle of "faith" mission cherished by the Pentecostal pioneers, Paul left the IPC to join Church of Christ, another foreign-funded venture, in 1959.[45] He established a congregation near Kakinada. Meanwhile, Venkata Ratnam Sade of Korukollu in the West Godavari district, a recent recruit in the IPC, joined the COG in 1960 and eventually became the principal of Pentecostal Bible School in Kakinada.[46]

Second, Peter Devasahayam Kanumala represents the loyal remnant in the IPC. While many of his colleagues left Samuel, Devasahayam remained in the denomination until he died in 1997. A Mala from Bhogapuram, Devasahayam was earlier associated with the Salvation Army and the CMS congregations consecutively. Attracted to its teachings, seventeen-year-old Devasahayam became a Pentecostal in 1950. After attending Zion Bible School for three years, he founded Pentecostal congregations in Madhavaram, Nidadavolu, and Upparagudem

---

44  *Gospel Illuminator* 35, no. 11 (November 1975): 7.

45  Rapaka, *Dalit Pentecostalism*, 71.

46  A telephone interview with Venkata Ratnam Sade on November 4, 2015.

in the West Godavari district. When Vedanayagam Sas-
try Tagaram left IPC in favor of WME, Samuel transferred
Devasahayam to Eluru in 1962.[47] Samuel rewarded Devasahayam's loyalty by funding an elementary school in Eluru.
Devasahayam later served prominent but nominal positions
at state and national levels. He was elected general secretary
of the Andhra IPC in 1975 and then vice president in 1993.
He served as its national vice president from 1996 until his
death the following year.

Third, even while faithfully serving their mother organization, some accessed overseas funding and directed it to their
families and friends. Paramjyothi, one of the IPC pioneers in
the state, loyally supported Samuel and warded off threats to
his dynasty. When offered financial support by Douglas, he rec-
ommended his student Samuel Godi as a possible beneficiary
in 1962.[48] The family members of Paramjyothi received from
Douglas financial support for their charitable activities. Samuel Godi led WME in India until Paramjyothi's descendants
unseated him in 1990.[49]

The spirit of assertion blew across in the COG as well. Taking advantage of missionaries' interest in caste Christians, Stephen Reddi, a Velama Christian and language teacher to the
Turners, rose to prominence and took over the administration
of the denomination in 1971, less than a decade after joining
the denomination.[50] He successfully engineered the eclipse of
Harold Turner, the resident American missionary, as well as that
of P. E. Varghese, a Malayalee preacher—a coup his senior

---

47  A telephone interview with Prasad Kumar Marlapudi on October 1,
    2015.
48  Rapaka, *Dalit Pentecostalism*, 80.
49  Bergunder, *South Indian Pentecostal Movement*, 98.
50  A telephone interview with Venkata Ratnam Sade on September 19,
    2015.

Dalit colleagues watched with dismay.[51] The change in leadership did not mean much to the Dalit pastors, as a "caste" leader took over from alien masters.

During this phase of rapid expansion, Pentecostal preachers sought shelter and support from Dalits in Protestant churches. Drawn to the message of spiritual empowerment and liturgical changes, Protestants, mostly women, provided the initial moral support to the preachers. For example, Satyavadhanamma, a Lutheran woman of Kamma caste, hosted Sudharshanam Chatla when he arrived in Rajanagaram in the East Godavari district.[52] Protestants welcomed the new preachers hoping for revivals within their congregations.[53] Housed in a Lutheran house, Sudharshanam organized revival meetings and invited Paramjyothi to introduce Pentecostal beliefs.

Aiming to Christianize caste families, Pentecostal preachers later moved from Dalit hamlets to Hindu neighborhoods. As part of the strategy, they erected church buildings in the caste neighborhoods to attract and accommodate Hindus. Simon Palivela, a COG pastor, pioneered a church in Gollaprolu in the East Godavari district and erected a worship center among the weaving community while his colleague Vijayaratnam Nadipalli constructed a church building among the landowning Kapu communities in Gorinta.[54] As mentioned at the beginning of this chapter, Dalit Christians subtly supported and many later remained in the Pentecostal churches. Some have returned to their mother churches.[55]

---

51  Bergunder, *South Indian Pentecostal Movement*, 99.

52  A telephone interview with Gabriel Chatla on September 18, 2015. Cf. Rapaka, *Dalit Pentecostalism*, 75.

53  There were numerous itinerant revival preachers in the liturgical churches as well during the period.

54  A telephone interview with Vijayaratnam Nadipalli on December 10, 2015.

55  A telephone interview with Prasad Kumar Marlapudi on October 10, 2015; and a telephone interview with Katuri David on October 10, 2015.

On the other hand, caste Christians often outnumbered their Dalit counterparts in the COG congregations. The COG congregation founded by Simon in Gollaprolu eventually became a Sali (a weaving community) congregation, and the one Vijayaratnam founded is dominated by Kapu Christians. The Maranatha Visvasa Samajam (MVS), which grew out of the COG in 1982, initially was a multicaste movement before becoming a Kamma denomination. These churches provided an opportunity for caste Hindus to embrace Christianity in a region where Protestantism was identified with Dalits.

### Consolidation of Caste Identities: 1981–Present

With the crystallization of caste-based polarities among the Telugus in the 1980s, the Pentecostal movement splintered further. Increasing access to foreign funding added to its divisions. The following three movements illustrate the dynamics of caste and economic control in its multiplication.

Samuel died in 1981. Two denominations grew out of the IPC thereafter. After Samuel's death, his office secretary Philip Papabathini (1936–2010), a Telugu pastor, wanted to succeed him, citing his "loyalty" to the founder and experience in administration. Meanwhile, Plathaneth Abraham Samuel claimed his right to succeed his father, as most Indian men do after their father's death.[56] Both claimants were experienced in ministry and administration. The feudal ecclesiology, a system in which congregations are considered inheritable personal properties, and the Keralite Pentecostals helped the grieving son's cause. The Malayalee leaders at the central office in Kerala favored Abraham Samuel, perhaps because of their shared linguistic

---

56 It is customary for Keralites to retain their father's second given name as their second given name.

identity. Paramjyothi, one of the local pioneers, supported Abraham Samuel. Philip was a Mala and Paramjyothi a Madiga, each belonging to two rival Dalit communities. Furious at the turn of events, Philip left the IPC (or was expelled) with his loyalists and founded Indian Pentecostal Community Church, with its headquarters in Chillakallu in the Guntur district.[57] The addition of "community" to the name of the new denomination signaled some degree of the assertion. By starting a new denomination, Philip and his new movement did challenge the Malayalee dominance in the Telugu Pentecostal movement.

While his cousin presided over a major split in and took over the reins of the IPC, Joseph Titus Puthenparampil returned to India in 1981. Born in 1935, Titus earlier worked with the IPC from 1955 in Hyderabad and Khammam until he left for the United States to pursue seminary education in 1965.[58] After sixteen years of residence in the United States, Titus returned to India with a renewed commitment to church ministry. Lest he further upset the power symmetry in the denomination, he approached it seeking "counsel and wisdom" on his next step in ministry. They swiftly and expectedly advised Titus to start his "own ministry" in a region where the IPC was absent or weaker, perhaps to minimize the threat to the Samuel dynasty.[59] As a result, Titus established the New Testament Church (NTC) and its affiliate Church on the Rock Seminary in Bheemunipatnam, north of Visakhapatnam. In terms of theology and polity, the NTC resembles its parent organization, the IPC. Both denominations were governed by Malayalee leaders, and most of their members were of Dalit descent.

---

57  Rapaka, *Dalit Pentecostalism*, 87.

58  Barbara Oldfield, *Dr. P. J. Titus: God's Man for India* (Bheemunipatnam, India: Church on the Rock, 1996), 12–22.

59  Joseph Titus Puthenparampil, "Pentecostal Indigenous Movements in Andhra," in *Christianity Is Indian: The Emergence of an Indigenous Community*, ed. Roger Hedlund (Delhi: ISPCK, 2000), 378.

Meanwhile, the COG experienced a major split when one of its leaders, Moses Choudary Gullapalli, parted ways and started the Maranatha Visvasa Samajam (MVS) in 1982. Social, economic, and theological factors contributed to the conflict between Reddi and Choudary. After completing his graduate program at Lee University, Choudary returned to his home denomination in India. The denominational headquarter in Cleveland, Tennessee, has an unwritten practice of appointing the alumni of Lee University as overseers to efficiently manage the administration of its branches across the world. With additional education and an extended network, Choudary returned home to play a larger role in the administration on the state level. He enthusiastically proposed administrative and ministerial reforms in the church. Choudary was critical of Reddi for holding the office of state representative indefinitely.[60] He also challenged his denomination's antagonism against local cultures.

Bergunder rightly identifies the influence of Donald A. McGavran, a church growth expert, on Choudary while the latter studied at Lee University. McGavran argued that the communities should be "discipled" as groups and claimed that dislocating them from their cultures impeded church growth.[61] Choudary wanted to appropriate McGavran's proposals in the COG, but the proposed reforms did not gain traction from the leadership, as they would undermine the long-cherished countercultural practices of the COG, such as the removal of jewelry by women. Choudary also called for a change in leadership. Reddi was not amused by the proposal. In response, Reddi accused Choudary of collecting funds for his personal use.[62] Disappointed at the lukewarm response of Reddi and his team, Choudary left the denomination with several pastors and rewarded them with

---

60 A telephone interview with Venkata Ratnam Sade on November 4, 2015.
61 Donald A. McGavran, *Church Growth: Strategies That Work* (Nashville, TN: Abingdon, 1980).
62 In a private conversation in the author's presence.

higher compensation. With pastors, congregations left. However, because of its ownership of the local church properties and the possibility of protracted legal battles, the official COG held its sway over the majority of the denomination.

As Bergunder points out, Choudary, a Kamma Christian, wanted to draw dominant caste Hindus toward Christianity and recognized that challenging their social practices would impede his mission. Caste, according to Choudary, is a social practice, and the gospel does not question this social mechanism.[63] With this core belief, the MVS had eventually become a Kamma movement and occupied the space left open after the eclipse of the Subba Rao movement, which we will discuss in the following chapter.

The early 1980s experienced the crystallization of caste-based polarities among the Telugus. This was a period when caste-based political parties, such as Telugu Desam Party, emerged, as did Mahanadu and Kapunadu, political platforms for caste communities. Nandamuri Taraka Rama Rao came to power highlighting the need for self-respect. Not immune to the churning caste consolidations, the Pentecostal movement splintered mostly on a caste basis. The churning caste polarization of Indian society after the Mandal movements in the early 1990s further associated congregations with caste identities. Prime Minister Morarji Desai of the Janata Party established a commission in 1979 to study the plight of the socially and educationally backward classes and to make recommendations for their welfare. Prime Minister Vishwanath Pratap Singh sought to implement the recommendations of the commission in 1990, resulting in a widespread agitation by caste communities either for or against its implementation.

Unlike other Pentecostal churches, the MVS encourages members to retain their pre-Christian names and highlight their

---

63 In a conversation with the author in 1990.

family names as a missionary strategy to convert their communities. Its worship and preaching patterns resemble those of Hindu *bhajans* to provide continuity with the pre-Christian culture of the dominant caste Christians. To protect the caste identities of the members, the MVS established a marriage bureau to guard the caste boundaries in marriage. Like other dominant caste matrimonial brokers, the bureau permits the practice of dowry and connects potential mates based on the color of their skin even within a caste.

What does the birth of the MVS mean to Telugu Pentecostalism? (1) The attitudes of Telugu Pentecostals toward pre-Christian cultures diversified. While the NTC, founded by Titus, retained its critical stance toward Telugu cultures, the MVS accommodated many of the local customs. For example, while classical Pentecostals fumed at jewelry as an abominable idol, the newer churches, like the MVS, allowed the wearing of jewelry. (2) The newer churches toned down the antielitist tendencies of the classical Pentecostals. The use of titles, such as "reverend" and "doctor," was once taboo, as classical Pentecostals viewed these titles as unbiblical. The newer churches enthusiastically embraced the titles of "reverend" and "doctor." (3) Earlier Pentecostals condemned the practice of caste within the church and underlined the spiritual fellowship of everyone baptized in the Holy Spirit. Parallel to the MVS ideology, numerous smaller and local denominations emerged on a caste basis. They preserved the caste distinctions, a survival strategy. Caste played a notoriously pivotal role in the power struggles in larger bodies, such as WME and the COG.

## Practices and Beliefs of the Telugu Pentecostals

The homogeneity of the Pentecostal communities makes the task of identifying common traits challenging. We shall, however, identify some of their practices and beliefs: First, like their

counterparts abroad, both classical and later Pentecostals promote the baptism in the Holy Spirit, the one that proceeds and
validates one's baptism in waters. Like their Baptist and Brethren
counterparts, Pentecostals insist on immersion, and in the case of
those baptized as infants, they do not mind requiring another ritual of baptism. While immersion baptism marks an individual's
decision to follow Jesus, baptism signifies God's acceptance of a
repenting individual. The latter is the beginning of the Holy Spirit's work of sanctification in an individual believer.

Second, Pentecostals employ the practice of fasting as a
means to invoke the infilling of the Holy Spirit. They cite the
Gospel story where Jesus is recorded to have fasted for forty
days (Matt 4:2). While some fast once a week, others undertake longer periods of fasting. The longer one fasts, the higher
one's standing in the community. Pentecostals believe fasting
provides a period of emptiness or temptation, a prerequisite for
empowerment by the Spirit.[64] When challenged and compared
to the Pharisaic practice of fasting, which Jesus is recorded to
have criticized, Pentecostals defend the practice as ordained by
Jesus.[65] Fasting and awaiting the infilling of the Spirit are thus
interrelated practices.

Third, classical Pentecostals view glossolalia as one of the
gifts of the Spirit. Though it is one of the many, it has been a
coveted gift and often is the marker to distinguish Pentecostals
from other Christians. Critics in the past argued that the gift of
speaking in unknown tongues is obsolete and, unaccompanied
by translation, is not edifying. In a brief written apologia for
glossolalia, Barnabas Kilari of Chittivalasa[66] identifies its biblical basis.[67] Barnabas ridicules Protestants and Catholics for

---

64  *Gospel Illuminator* 39, no. 7 (July 1979): 9.

65  *Gospel Illuminator*, 9.

66  Barnabas is the father of K. A. Paul, a televangelist located in Houston,
Texas.

67  *Gospel Illuminator* 35, no. 12 (November 1975): 7.

relegating the gift to the past, citing the Telugu proverb "Sour are inaccessible grapes." He argues the gift of speaking in unrecognizable tongues is still relevant today and is valid even without translation to the native tongue. Barnabas encourages his critics to earnestly and prayerfully seek the gift.

In a typical Pentecostal style, Barnabas cushions his argument with biblical verses. First, God promises the Spirit and the gift of glossolalia to believers of all ages and continents. God is trustworthy and never makes empty promises. Barnabas cites the sermon of Peter (Acts 2:39) where the preacher explains the commotion on the day of Pentecost as the fulfillment of God's promise of the Spirit. Second, Jesus, according to Luke (Acts 2:4), commends his disciples to wait for the descent of the Spirit. This, according to Barnabas, is an eternally relevant command for all God's people. Third, Barnabas concludes that the ability to speak in unknown tongues is a sure and visible sign of the Spirit Baptism. He bases his argument on 1 Corinthians 14:22 and Mark 16:1–20. Barnabas, however, conveniently ignores other signs in the same passages. Published in the official newsletter of the Telugu wing of the IPC, this sermon reflects the Pentecostal perceptions about glossolalia.

Pentecostals, however, later softened their stance, as many children in the Pentecostal families could not or did not try to speak in unknown tongues. Some have even questioned the prescribed exercises that preachers used to enable people to speak in unrecognizable languages.[68] There might be subtle differences of opinion about glossolalia, but no Pentecostal denies its relevance today.

Fourth, Pentecostals encourage lay apostolate. Citing the proverbial saying "Shepherds do not give birth to lambs, but sheep do," Eliah Taneti, a COG pastor in Samarlakota, often prodded his congregation members to introduce the Christian

---

68 A telephone interview with Venkata Ratnam Sade on November 4, 2015.

faith to their families and neighbors and invite them to faith in Christ. While members find fulfillment in the number of individuals they bring to the church, pastors pride themselves on numbering the congregations they establish. In my encounters and telephone interviews with Pentecostal pastors, they fondly introduced themselves with the names of places where they founded congregations.[69]

Fifth, given their roots in the modern missionary movement and worldwide revivals, Pentecostals anticipate an unannounced end to history.[70] Their belief in premillennialism provides an impetus behind the modern missions.[71] They believe that Christ will return to earth and usher in a millennial rule, but that will not come to pass until the gospel is introduced to everyone on earth. This belief enthused the nineteenth-century missionaries to engage in worldwide evangelism. Like their spiritual ancestors, Pentecostals seek to hasten the return of Christ and his millennial rule by spreading their faith. Citing 2 Thessalonians 2:3, they encourage congregations to recapture the spirit of anticipation for the "coming day" from the early church.[72] With the "end" in mind, they invite Christians to receive two baptisms, one of immersion in waters and another in the Holy Spirit. Turning outside the church, Pentecostals invite their non-Christian neighbors to have faith in Christ. This sense of apocalyptic urgency and hope for the millennial role fan the missionary zeal of Telugu Pentecostals.

---

69 In his fifty-six years of pastoral ministry, David Brainard Beera of Amalapuram established churches in twenty-four villages, according to an email communication with Manohar James on October 23, 2015. These numbers fit well in the pattern, especially in the first two periods.

70 Michael Bergunder, "Constructing Indian Pentecostalism," in *Asian and Pentecostal: The Charismatic Face of Christianity in Asia*, ed. Allen Anderson and Edmond Tang, Regnum Studies in Mission, 2nd ed. (Eugene, OR: Wipf & Stock, 2011), 146.

71 Bergunder, 147.

72 *Gospel Illuminator* 35, no. 7 (July 1975): 4.

With this enthusiasm, some preachers crossed the seas as missionaries. For example, John Sundara Rao of Movva in the Krishna district left for the islands of Andaman as a missionary in 1975.[73] With a bachelor of science degree, Sundara Rao had earlier worked in the publication department of the IPC in Vijayawada. A year later, another Telugu preacher, K. Balidhanam, went to a different community in the islands as a missionary but returned home the same year.[74] The monthly newsletter of the IPC, the *Gospel Illuminator*, celebrated these missionary travels and underlined the missional calling of the church.[75]

Sixth, the practice of testimonies opens more opportunities for the lay—male and female—to lead the worship. During the worship services, there is a designated time for worshippers to share their "testimonies." In weekly worship, where most of those present are Christian, testimonies recount what God was doing in one's life. Lay members share matters of joy and concern. They solicit praise and prayers on their behalf. In the presence of non-Christian neighbors, these testimonies recall how the speaker was drawn to Christianity, aiming to invite the auditors to the new faith. On both occasions, women speakers confidently cite biblical verses and, through their stories, subtly interpret them.

Seventh, insisting on a life of simplicity, classical Pentecostals consistently condemn the wearing of jewelry. They buttress this practice by citing the story from Exodus 32:1–6, in which Hebrew travelers, under the leadership of Aaron, make a golden calf and worship it, thereby invoking God's anger. In an article written in *Suvartha Prakashini*, the official magazine of the IPC, the writer traces the beginning of the practice of wearing

---

73  *Gospel Illuminator* 35, no. 9 (September 1975): 7. A telephone interview with John Sunder Rao on October 12, 2015.

74  *Gospel Illuminator* 36, no. 11 (November 1976): 14.

75  *Gospel Illuminator*, 14.

jewelry to the veneration of the golden calf.[76] The author claims God through Moses commands the Hebrew slaves to melt the golden calf and offer it at the altar. Women members are therefore called to shun their jewelry and, if possible, present it in the offertory plates. The removal of jewelry, they also argue, distinguishes them from their caste counterparts.[77]

However, the renunciation of gold had debilitating implications for women. Not all women possessed golden jewelry. Gold was the only commodity women could control, their only bargaining weapon. Women inherited it from their maternal ancestors and utilized it when a need arose. The requirement to abandon golden jewelry may have denied them a social bargaining tool. The later Pentecostal churches—such as the MVS and especially those born after the 1980s—allow the wearing of jewelry.

## How Indigenous Is Telugu Pentecostalism?

In his study of Indian-initiated churches, Roger Hedlund, a missionary-scholar, characterizes Pentecostal churches as Indigenous. In a project conducted in the late 1990s, when majoritarian fundamentalists in India pigeonholed Christianity as an alien religion, Hedlund eagerly caricatures Pentecostals as truly indigenous. This caricature is accurate if indigeneity is limited to the native agency in establishing these churches. If we are to account for theology, financial support, and governance, this claim to Pentecostal indigeneity cannot be sustained. A careful examination of the self-propagation, self-theologizing, self-governance, and self-support of Telugu Christians would illumine the tradition's indigeneity.

76 *Gospel Illuminator* 34, no. 8 (August 1974): 13.
77 *Gospel Illuminator* 36, no. 12 (December 1976): 3.

The process of transmission and appropriation belonged primarily to the native Pentecostals. At the level of preparation for ministry, Malayalee missionaries have significantly impacted the theological formation of the Telugu pastors and, through them, their congregations. The training schools in Gunadala, Kakinada, and Bheemunipatnam provided Malayalee missionaries the chance to shape the appropriation of the Pentecostal thought in the region at least until 1980. Yearly, Pentecostals from the United States and European countries visited and preached at large conventions to relentlessly moor the local theologies to their brand of Pentecostalism. However, it was Telugus who articulated Pentecostal theology in song and sermon daily in Telugu.

Does the use of Telugu alone make Pentecostal theology indigenous? Titus, the founder of Church on the Rock Seminary, concludes in the negative. He rightly identifies the imprints of foreign theologies on the local Pentecostalism. First, the theology of the Cyrus I. Scofield Reference Bible, published in 1909, "influenced" the eschatology of Telugu Pentecostals.[78] Second, Telugu Pentecostals inherited the use of typologies, dispensationalist theology, and premillennialism from their American counterparts.[79] Third, Telugu Pentecostals' emphasis on another world and obsession with holiness can be traced to Reuben A. Torrey and Albert B. Simpson, ideologues of the Christian and Missionary Alliance. Fourth, I add, a significant number of Bible studies, sermons, and biographies in their monthly magazines were translated from their counterparts in the United States.[80]

Where do Pentecostal congregations receive their funding from? Local congregation members and well-wishers largely contribute to the church treasuries through their offerings—cash and kind. Citing the biblical principle of workers' rights over

---

78  Puthenparampil, "Pentecostal Indigenous Movements," 368.

79  Puthenparampil, 368.

80  *Gospel Illuminator* 34, no. 10 (October 1974): 5.

their wages, Pentecostal pastors solicit offerings from their congregation members and take complete charge of the income.
They use their "wages" at their discretion, mostly to meet
their personal needs and occasionally for the ministries of their
churches. In most cases, pastors pay one-tenth of the income to
denominational headquarters.

Funding from overseas is another significant source of
income. Donations come with strings attached—at least con-
cerning how the money ought to be spent. With the funds
received abroad, denominational bodies partially contribute to
the living expenses of the pastors and their ministerial needs.
Most foreign funding ordinarily is designated for the construction of sanctuaries and maintenance of homes for orphans
and schools for the destitute. The discretion to distribute the
funds is vested in the denominational headquarters. Of course,
those with familiarity with English and overseas networks can
bypass the processes. A hint of assertion or disloyalty often
results in the loss of foreign funding. Thus the reliance on funding from outside sources that decide the local needs and the
ways to cater to these needs problematizes calling these congregations or denominations self-supporting churches.

The countercultural stance of Pentecostal preachers is evident in their earlier refusal to use ecclesiastical and academic
titles, such as "reverend" and "doctor." According to a writer in
*Suvartha Prakashini*, God alone deserves to be revered.[81] As such, no
human being—clergy or lay—is worthy of the title "reverend."
Moreover, the author argues, the titles "reverend" and "doctor" are not biblical, as they are not listed among the ministries
recorded in Ephesians 4:8–15.[82] The use of such titles, according
to the author, is an attempt at self-glorification and amounts to
idolatry, with a human seeking glory designated only to God.

---

81  *Gospel Illuminator* 35, no. 5 (July 1975): 5.
82  *Gospel Illuminator* 37, no. 7 (July 1977): 11.

What has Pentecostalism done to the Telugu Church? First, with their teachings about the Holy Spirit, Telugu Pentecostals accentuated the work of the Holy Spirit in the ministry of the church and the lives of individual Christians. According to John Billa, a Telugu theologian, the theology of the Telugus is so lopsided that only two persons in the Trinity feature in the Telugu Christian hymnal, and only seven hymns directly embed the theme of the Trinity.[83] Two of the seven are translated from the English language. The Bible Mission, which is discussed in chapter 7, emerged as a response to this theological imbalance. The emergence of movements such as the Bible Mission and that of Subba Rao Kalagara attests to Pentecostals' impact on the Telugu Church.

Second, Pentecostal churches prodded Telugu Christians to become outward looking in an era when Christianity had become an inherited identity. After the massive Dalit conversions, congregations, by and large, were caste based. Pentecostalism has inspired Dalit Christians to reach beyond their hamlets and invite others to faith in Christ. This missionary consciousness ultimately contributed to the social diversification of the Telugu Church.

Third, Pentecostals enriched the Telugu Christians' belief in the ministry of Christ. Importing restoration theologies from the United States, they brought to the Telugu Christian community the notion of Christ not only as savior but also as healer, sanctifier, and the Coming King.[84]

Fourth, Pentecostal claims of unmediated access to the Spirit often trumped the educational qualifications of the Protestant ministers, and their spontaneity undermined the prepared liturgies of the mainstream churches. These extraordinary experiences

---

83  A telephone interview with John Billa on December 12, 2020.
84  Anderson and Tang, *Asian and Pentecostal.*

allowed women and men alike to speak for the divine, a practice that resonates with Dalit worship patterns.

Lastly, in addition to being countercultural, Pentecostal theologies have often been otherworldly. The songs they introduced—like "Siyonu Patalu Santhoshamula Paduchu Siyonu Velludhamu" (Let us go to Zion singing joyfully the songs of Zion) and "Paravasini e Jagamuna Prabhuva Nadacuchunnanu Dharini" (Alien I am on the earth, I am on way, O Lord!)—contributed to the otherworldly orientation of the Telugu Church.

With its emphasis on the Spirit, personal holiness, and otherworldliness, Pentecostalism was not an anomaly. It had its cousins both in challenging the forms of Christianity reminiscent of the colonial period and in creating new theological trajectories. These indigenizing tendencies were present in all traditions dating back to the colonial era, which we will study now.

# 6

# Consolidated Centers and Expansive Edges

The middle of the twentieth century marked the birth of modern India, with the British colonial powers leaving the subcontinent and handing over their reins to the Indian National Congress in 1947. The political map of India dramatically transformed thereafter. Under attack from the Indian Union armies, the nizam of Hyderabad surrendered his dominion. Fueled by the struggles for a single state on a linguistic basis, the Indian Union formed the state of Andhra Pradesh in 1956, stitching together territories from the Madras Presidency, Hyderabad, and other princely states. The transfer of power and the formation of greater Andhra Pradesh in the middle of the twentieth century coincided with the consolidation of confessional churches and the expansion of the locally initiated movement. The CSI, which included five Telugu-speaking dioceses, was formed in 1947. The following decade witnessed the flourishing of eclectic movements led by Devadas Mungamuri (Father M. Devadas), Bakht Singh Chabra (Brother Bakht Singh), and Subba Rao Kalagara, a phenomenon that Roger Hedlund calls "Little Traditions." In this chapter, I discuss the transformation of Telugu Christianity in the postcolonial era.

I hesitate to distinguish Telugu churches as denominational and indigenous, as all movements in independent India have eventually become denominations. For example, the Hebron movement, also called Bakht Singh Fellowship, depended on the guidance of its founder until his death. Singh, at his discretion, appointed professional ministers in "assemblies" and transferred them at his will. Local elders directly negotiated with him about their needs and interests. The full-time ministers who refused to heed his orders found themselves out of the movement. On the other hand, the CSI operated on a blended constitution, an improvised version of Congregational, Presbyterian, and Episcopal polities. This improvisation was necessitated by the local needs, especially the need for a national united church in the postcolonial era. The difference between the so-called mission churches and their local counterparts is that the former is governed (or at least guided) by a written constitution, while the latter is directed by their leaders' discretion.

Calling some global and others local is also problematic, as such clean distinctions deface the local roots and global networks of each. With an exception of the Bible Mission, every movement was globally connected. British colonial officials left in 1947, but the Western missionaries did not. They remained in the churches and mission institutions founded during the colonial period despite the struggles for and promises of devolution of power. Western missionaries governed some of the CSI dioceses. Even after the devolution of power, the AELC elected Samuel W. Schmittenner as its president between 1969 and 1981. The church associated with Lutheran entities abroad, while the CSI joined the Anglican Communion and global Reformed coalitions. Pentecostal and Holiness churches were no exception. They wholeheartedly welcomed and allied with churches and leaders in North America and Europe. For example, John E. Douglas Sr. was the director of WME, and Harold Turner controlled the COG (Andhra Pradesh) until 1971. At Hebron, Singh hosted Western missionaries.

Telugu churches of all theological shades are indigenous not only because of local or improvised polities but also because of their roots. In other words, all churches in the region are Telugu-initiated churches. As demonstrated in the earlier chapters, it was natives who approached the Western missionaries asking to be baptized and catechized, and it was again the native Christians who introduced their newly found faith to their religious neighbors and catechized the nascent Christians. Thus the liturgical churches are as native as the free churches, as they have drawn extensively from the inspiration and perspiration of the local agency.

Both denominational and free churches drew extensively from theological resources from abroad. During the embryonic phase of the CSI, the union negotiations worked around four basic convictions adapted from the Lambeth Conference, which I shall list later in the chapter.[1] Telugu evangelical Lutherans subscribed to the theological underpinnings of Martin Luther, a German Reformer. In their understandings and interpretations of the Scriptures, Pentecostal preachers followed the restoration theologies of A. J. Simpson,[2] while the Hebron churches appropriated the Keswickian ecclesiology.[3] While acknowledging the overlaps and subtle differences, I will discuss in this chapter the continued process of contextualization in the liturgical churches and their theological education.

## Ecumenical Adventures

What was happening to the church at large? The second half of the nineteenth century ushered in an era of missionary cooperation, and the notion of ecumene came into existence

---

1 Bengt Sundkler, *Church of South India: The Movement towards Union, 1900–1947* (London: Lutterworth, 1965), 23.

2 Puthenparampil, "Pentecostal Indigenous Movements," 377.

3 Evangeline Bharathi Nuthalapati, *Brother Bakht Singh: Theologian and Father of the Indian Independent Christian Church Movement* (Carlisle, UK: Langham Monographs, 2017), 38.

at the dawn of the century. The principles of comity in the
mission contexts enabled missionaries of disparate confessional
backgrounds to imagine broader cooperation. The decennial
conferences that began on the subcontinent in the middle of
the nineteenth century found parallels not only in other mission contexts but also in the North Atlantic world. Missionaries of different Protestant denominations gathered during the
summer months every ten years to spend time together, discuss
their missionary strategies, and worship together.[4] Meanwhile,
the mission bureaucrats in Europe and North America gathered
on both sides of the Atlantic to find ways to efficiently use their
resources and support their missionaries working abroad. The
word *ecumene* entered the Christian diction at one of such international missionary conferences that met in New York in 1900.[5]
These gatherings eventually culminated in the famous World
Missionary Conference in Edinburgh in 1910, which was the
birthplace of the International Missionary Council, Faith and
Order, and Life and Work movements. The latter two joined to
form the World Council of Churches in 1948.

In the aftermath of the Edinburgh 1910 conference, ecumenical leaders organized national missionary councils in mission
contexts. To promote cooperation and efficiently share resources,
Protestant denominations established joint ventures in the fields
of theological education, health, and higher learning. The United
Theological College, Arogyavaram Medical Center, and Vellore
Christian Mission Center—founded in 1910, 1915, and 1917,
respectively—are fruits of such missionary cooperation.

Meanwhile, representatives from the South India United
Church—a union of Congregationalists, Presbyterians, and Angli-
cans from Jaffna formed in 1908—welcomed the Malabar-based

---

4  R. Pierce Beaver, *Ecumenical Beginnings in Protestant World Mission: A History
   of Comity* (New York: Thomas Nelson & Sons, 1962), 66–72.

5  Ruth Rouse and Stephen Charles Neill, eds., *A History of the Ecumenical
   Movement: 1517–1948* (Geneva: World Council of Churches, 1986), 1:354.

Basel Mission in 1919, providing a model for an organic union. Assisted by resident Western missionaries, a group of Indian clergy—including Vedanayagam Samuel Azariah, a Tamil missionary in Dornakal, initiated conversations on the possible organic union.[6] The South India United Church in Tranquebar, Anglican dioceses in India, and Wesleyan Methodist missionaries joined the table. Given the rich theological diversity and complex differences in the polity, they needed a theological base for the union negotiations. They borrowed the Lambeth Quadrilateral from 1888 as a basic guiding document. The negotiating churches were to agree on the following four convictions. They are (1) the Old and New Testaments as sufficient for salvation, (2) the Apostles' and Nicene Creeds as the minimal theological bases, (3) baptism and the Lord's Supper as the two sacraments, and (4) the local appropriation of episcopacy. To continue the conversation, they formed a Joint Committee with delegates from each of the denominations at the table.

In the twenty-eight-year-long union conversation, other confessional bodies joined and left for both theological and practical reasons. The Joint Committee had succeeded in publishing the Scheme Union after the decade long negotiation. The question was not on which of the Quadrilateral principles to be retained but on how to interpret each. Defining the Lord's Supper has been a hurdle, but the attempt to contextual the historic episcopacy was a bigger obstacle. The negotiating parties had to deliberate on a governing structure that was relevant, pragmatic, and yet respectful of the traditions in a possible union. While retaining episcopacy, the newly drafted constitution allowed more bargaining space for presbyters and congregations. Lay members elected by the congregation and presbyters participated in the governance. It was also necessitated by the

---

6  Billington Harper's book *In the Shadow of the Mahatma* interprets the leadership and legacy of Vedanayagam Samuel Azariah.

prospect of a bishop from one of the traditions imposing their decisions—theological and administrative—on a congregation from another tradition. For example, while the bishop had the right to appoint a minister over a congregation, the latter had the power to decline the appointment. Appointed presbyters had the opportunity to accept or reject an appointment to serve a congregation they were not theologically at home with. This arrangement was provisional as the negotiating partners began to live into the unity, but it also attests to the pastoral and theological sensitivity in matters of polity. Thus these negotiations and the arrangements made thereof addressed the contextual realities of the subcontinent for a united national church. Although the union negotiations occurred in the colonial context, they envisioned a church that not only was united but also accommodated local needs and interests.

The drafted constitution came into effect on September 17, 1947, with the laying on of hands on the elected bishops and presbyteries.[7] With more than a million members, the nascent CSI included Tamil, Kannadiga, Malayalam, and Telugu churches.[8] At the time of its inception, five Telugu-speaking dioceses were formed, and for two of them, Telugu bishops were consecrated. At the consecration service held at St. George's Cathedral in Chennai, in a ceremony of the mutual laying on of hands, a ritual designed to affirm the validity of ministry of all participating churches, Muthyalu Yeddu was consecrated as the bishop of the Krishna-Godavari diocese and Joseph Bunyan as the bishop of the Kurnool and Anantapur diocese.[9] H. Sumitra, a Kannadiga, was appointed to lead the diocese of Kadapa and Chittoor, while A. B. Elliot and F. Whittaker to were appointed to shepherd the dioceses of Dornakal and Hyderabad.

7  Sundkler, *Church of South India*, 344.

8  K. M. George, *Church of South India: Life in Union, 1947–1997* (Delhi: ISPCK, 1999), 23.

9  George, 17.

At the local level, popular piety flourished and was subtly permitted. The rituals both the members and the pilgrims engaged in attested to the indigeneity within the CSI. Studying the annual Jathara, a folk religious fair, at Luxettipet, CSI pastorate in the Adilabad district Vasantha Rao Chilkuri identifies the continuity of Indigenous practices within the church.[10] Vasantha Rao construes these fairs as opportunities to share Christian beliefs. Hailing from the same diocese, Zaccheaus Katta, another CSI minister, studies the popular folk practices at the Medak Cathedral. He identifies at least six rites he observed.[11] The Medak Cathedral, a ten-year-long construction project, was open for worship by 1924. This shrine brings together people from several regions in South India, especially from Hindu backgrounds. First, considering it a sacred site, people of all religious persuasions undertake pilgrimages (*tirtha yatra*) to the cathedral. While the parish members worship and observe the practices of baptism and the Lord's Table on Sundays, pilgrims throng to the shrine any day of the week. They do so seeking the vision or the sight (*darśana*) of God and personal well-being, such as healing or prosperity or social respect. Second, in fulfilling the vows they made, some of them bring and sacrifice sheep or chicken, mostly before sunrise. Katta observes that these sacrifices are offered especially during the liturgical seasons of Advent or Holy Week.[12] Third, the visiting pilgrims take a ritual bath before sunrise in a water tank that the church has built for the purpose.[13] The cathedral authorities play recorded devotional songs with

---

10  Vasantha Rao Chilkuri, *Jathara: A Festival of Christian Witness* (Delhi: ISPCK, 1997).

11  Zaccheaus Katta, "Significance of Rituals Practiced by Hindus in CSI Medak Cathedral in Andhra Pradesh" (BD thesis, United Theological College, India, 2001).

12  Katta, 12.

13  Katta, 12–13.

loudspeakers to heighten the sense of sacredness, just as Hindu temple officials do. Fourth, almost all pilgrims break coconuts at the right side of the cathedral entrance, a Hindu practice of libation.[14] Many Christians break coconuts at the time of groundbreaking and housewarming as well. Fifth, parents bring their newly born before they turn a year old and tonsure their hair, a Hindu practice of purification.[15] This practice emerges from the popular belief that having inhabited the mother's womb, every child is defiled and therefore ought to be purified. Some adults offer their hair as a promised return for the "divine" favors they received. Sixth, some pilgrims touch the holy ground with their hands in reverence and touch their heads with the same hands. A few others circumambulate the cathedral before entering.[16]

## Confessional Consolidations

The efforts to form national churches based on confessional identity paralleled the negotiations for a structural union. As part of such efforts, Lutheran missionaries of mission agencies together formed the AELC in 1927. In the sphere of ministerial training, Lutherans, Baptists, Methodists, and the CSI started collaborating in training native clergy in 1964. Even while retaining some level of clergy formation in their respective seminaries in Gooty, Nandyala, Dornakal, Ramayapatnam, Kakinada, and Rajahmundry, these churches cooperated on advanced ministerial formation in Rajahmundry first and then eventually moved their seminary to Hyderabad, its current location, in 1973. As a Protestant ecumenical seminary, the participating churches nominate the teaching staff and recruit students. The administration of the seminary is rotated

14  Katta, 14.
15  Katta, 14.
16  Katta, 15.

among the faculties of each participating body. The seminary has been the mainstay of ministerial formation within the confessional churches and occasionally beyond.

Meanwhile, St. John's Regional Seminary was relocated to Hyderabad in 1965. Founded by the Mill Hill Missionaries, its origins date back to 1883. There was a thirty-year pause of its training program before it reopened in 1924 in Nellore.[17] Minor seminaries in Eluru, Nellore, Khammam, and Bheemunipatnam continued their clergy training programs.

In the second half of the twentieth century, Venkata Subbamma Bathineni, a Lutheran minister, moved what was predominantly a Dalit church toward Sanskritization. The signs of deliberate efforts to incorporate the local idioms into the traditional faith in the Telugu Lutheran church date to the first half of the twentieth century, which we will discuss in the next chapter. For now, we shall discuss the Ashram movement of Subbamma, who remained in the AELC and sought changes.

Subbamma, a Kamma Christian and a contemporary of Subba Rao Kalagara, established ashrams for women, which she called "Pathana [study] Paricharya [service] Ashram."[18] At the gradual eclipse of Biblewomen training, she located her activities at the Charlotte Swenson Memorial Bible Training School in Luthergiri in Rajahmundry since 1968. The school, of which Subbamma was the principal, had earlier trained Biblewomen. As the name of the Ashram movement suggests, these centers were after the Hindu communities of learning and service. By 1971, there were ashrams in Rajahmundry, Peddapuram, Kakinada, Chirala, and Bhimavaram.

---

17  For more about the clergy training by the Mill Hill Missionaries, see John Rooney, *Of Ground Broken* (Bombay, India: St. Paul's Training School, 1995), 134–36.

18  Venkata Subbamma Bathineni, *Christ Confronts India: Indigenous Expression of Christianity in India* (Madras, India: Diocesan, 1973), 83.

These ashrams were designed for "newly baptized women converts" of dominant caste origins to Christianity.[19] At these ashrams, the emphasis had been on teaching the *paricharakulu* (deaconesses) the indigenous methods of communication, grooming women's leadership, forging conversations with Hindus, serving the communities, empowering the women with skills needed for self-reliance, and introducing Christianity to non-Christian neighbors.[20] Subbamma's call for indigenization presumes a degree of alienness that she found in the church, which was predominantly Dalit but had appropriated the lifestyles and beliefs of the American missionaries to distinguish itself from other indigenous cultures. Consisting of women from non-Dalit backgrounds, the Ashram movement had guided the AELC at least in the last three decades of the twentieth century toward Sanskritization even while retaining the office of deaconess from Europe.

There was a similar movement, but that one, led by Abel Boanerges Masilamani (1914–90), synthesized bhakti and evangelicalism through song. Hymns played a vital part in the formation of Telugu Christian thought. Theologians with the abilities to compose and sing make more of an optimal impact than those who write prose. As mentioned earlier, beliefs, for Telugus, are often preserved, expressed, and celebrated in the spoken word. Hymns function as catechetical tools.

Born in a mission hospital compound, Masilamani grew up as a Baptist. His mother, Saramma Boanerges, was a schoolteacher and a Biblewoman as well. As expected of her roles, she also preached and modeled the Christian faith. Masilamani's father, Gershon Paul Boanerges, was a male nurse at Christian Medical Centre in Pithapuram. Thus the family was located right amid the Christian community and was immersed in the Baptist tradition. After completing high school in Samarlakota, Masilamani

---

19  Bathineni, *Ashram*, 14.
20  Bathineni, *Christ Confronts*, 86. Cf. Bathineni, *Ashram*, 17–18.

pursued basic training at Baptist Theological Seminary in Kakinada, where he studied under Bhanumurti Chetti, another prolific hymn writer. It is not surprising that in a seminary consisting predominantly of Dalits, Masilamani, a Visva Brahmin (goldsmith), and Bhanumurti, a Vaishya (of the merchant community), bonded well. Given their social locations and upbringings, they shared a love for classical Telugu prose and music. Bhanumurti, who also ministered at the adjacent Baptist church located in Kakinada, composed several heart-touching hymns, seventeen of which are sung even today. Masilamani's interest in theater and music matured at the seminary, making him a prolific hymn writer and eloquent preacher. Masilamani eventually pursued graduate and doctoral studies in Canada and India.

The beginnings of his ministry coincided with the formation of erstwhile Andhra Pradesh.[21] He first ministered in the Convention of Baptist Churches in the Northern Circars in the 1950s and 1960s and later with New Life Associates, which he founded in 1970 and served until he died in 1990. In addition to his hymns and sermons, he wrote short books and also published a popular magazine, *Kapari* (Shepherd), a preaching resource for the Telugu clergy. With his versatile gifts, Masilamani profoundly shaped the faith of Telugu Christians for more than four decades in postcolonial India.

Masilamani's flair with wordplay continued late into his life, resulting in forty-four hymns, ten of which are listed in the Telugu Christian hymnal.[22] He continued the legacy of dominant castes impacting the translation of the Christian faith. In addition to writing his own, Masilamani also translated English

---

21  The greater Andhra Pradesh was bifurcated into the states of Andhra Pradesh and Telangana in 2014.

22  Ranjit Kumar Kanithi, "The Elements of Bhakti in the Lyrics of Acharya A. B. Masilamani: Its Implications for Mission and Its Relevance to the Convention of Baptist Churches in the Northern Circars" (MTh thesis, Serampore University, 2005), 45.

hymns—such as "Blest Be the Tie That Binds" by John Faw-
cett, a first-generation British evangelical—thus ensuring the
Telugu Christians' continued connection with evangelical tradition. While most of Purushotham Chowdhari's songs were
composed as responses to faith crises or in the context of street
preaching, most of Masilamani's hymns were written for huge
gatherings of Telugu Christians who assembled in Vijayawada
annually under the auspices of the Andhra Christian Council.
A gifted preacher, Masilamani used his skills and the opportunities they afforded him to shape Telugu Christian beliefs. He
enhanced the effect of his sermons by composing and teaching hymns to his audience, committing his theology to their
memories. Most of his hymns thus functioned as catechetical
tools. By nature, these annual gatherings were ecumenical, with
attendance from many Protestant traditions. The collaboration
of preachers from the CSI, AELC, and Baptist churches necessitated a theology that was less polemic and more conciliatory.
Not all Masilamani's songs were composed for these ecumenical gatherings, but he might well have had multidenomina-
tional audiences in mind in writing all of his hymns.

Given the audience and changed political context, one can
see a remarkable shift in the tone and texture of Baptist theological discourse. Although Masilamani was closely associated
with Canadian missionaries, his audience was Telugu in postcolonial India. Most of his auditors were second-generation
converts to Christianity. The initial controversies between
Protestant missionaries had focused on the choice of words for
baptism in the Telugu translation of the Bible.[23] Americus V.
Timpany, a Canadian Baptist missionary, challenged John Hay
of the LMS and the Madras Auxiliary Bible Society for their
choice of the Telugu word for baptism. Translating for the

---

23 Americus V. Timpany, *The Bible: A Reply to a Tract Written by the Rev. J. Hay, M.A.,
    Waltair, Madras Presidency, India* (Toronto: Baptist Publishing, 1878).

Bible Society, Hay translated *baptism* as "cleansing," while Timpany preferred the Telugu word for immersion. The Telugu preachers in independent India composed songs and evolved doctrines that were sensitive to the changing needs of the church and more conciliatory.

If the theology of Masilamani were to be seen as a window into Telugu Christian thought in the latter half of the twentieth century, how would that be? Telugu Christians in the postdenominational era moved to a christocentric theology. The questions of doctrinal intricacies gave way to explaining who Christ was. Telugu preachers introduced Christ as the only avatar (visible personification) of God, in contrast to the possibility of many avatars that Vishnavite Hindus believed. This is evident in Masilamani's hymns.

The accent on one personal and visible God emerged out of the bhakti tradition, as did the genre used to articulate this Christology. Telugus have been singing praises of their *ista dhaivam* (a beloved God / a God of choice) since the sixteenth century. Ratna Sundara Rao Rayi, in his illuminating book *Telugulo Chraistava Sahityam* (Christian literature in Telugu), analyzes the prominence of music in bhakti tradition and how pervasive that tradition was in Telugu Christian hymns.[24] Ranjit Kumar Kanithi, the principal of Baptist Theological Seminary in Kakinada, concurs with Sundara Rao and highlights the influences of bhakti in Telugu hymnody.[25]

Given the bhakti influences on Telugu Christian piety, Christ became the object of worship, an avatar of God. In a song that narrates the conversation between Jesus and two convicts on the cross (Luke 23:39–43), Masilamani interprets Jesus as the face of God. Masilamani believes that in the emaciated countenance of the crucified Jesus, humanity can see

24  Rayi, *Telugulo Chraistava Sahityam*, xxi.
25  Kanithi, "Elements of Bhakti," 36–42.

God revealed. Given their daily experiences of servitude and forced labor, this portrait of God in the crucified Christ would have appealed to Telugu Christians, most of whom were Dalits. Goddesses in the Dalit pantheon often were victims of rape or murder before being deified by the Dalit community.

One of Masilamani's hymns highlights the pathos of God:

*In the face (countenance) of Jesus, I see my God [My God revealed Godself]*
*Grace was poured out at Calvary to redeem the sinner*
*My soul yearned for heaven and eternal life*
*In the face (countenance) of Jesus, I see my God*

*Involved in wickedness and brutality,*
*I wandered in all directions with the weight of my sin*
*In the face (countenance) of Jesus, I see my God*

*Greedy after money and with animal instincts,*
*I deteriorated towards the ebbs of death*
*In the face (countenance) of Jesus, I see my God*

*Kindly remember me, Jesus, when you arrive with your kingdom on earth*
*I plead and weep, hear my plea*
*In the face (countenance) of Jesus, I see my God*

*You will partake in the other world today with joy*
*I journey towards the Lord with heaven as my last breath*
*In the face (countenance) of Jesus, I see my God.*[26]

Masilamani further explicates his Christology in a hymn entitled "Yesu Kristu Dhevudu," which means "Jesus Christ is

---

26 *Andhra Chraistava Keertanalu*, 545–46; translations from this work are my own.

Lord." The recurring prelude to the song sums up not only Masilamani's Christology but also that of many Telugu Christians:

*Jesus Christ is the Son of God*
*Jesus Christ is the Son of Man*
*Jesus Christ is God; Jesus is Lord*
*He is worthy to be praised*

*The power of God's righteousness is manifest in Jesus' cross*
*The image of God of gods is in the name of Jesus*
*Priceless is the Word of Yahweh; a delight to God's people*

*[Jesus is] the glory without ends*
*An incarnation of God who carries our burdens*
*The lord of heavens and celestial beings*

*The source of universal creativity*
*The giver and head of the entire world*
*The generous giver of grace every day*

*[Jesus is] the name the sin is afraid of*
*An offering of grace to the sinner*
*The voice of love to the seeking humanity*

*An offer of heavenly bliss*
*A song of forgiveness of sin*
*A gift of strength and the true sacrifice*

*[Jesus is] the lord of people's life*
*The light that rules the world*
*The final judge of all the living*
*The victor who conquered life and death*

*The flame that transforms the evil world.*[27]

Drawing from the titles used for Jesus in the Gospels, Masilamani presents Jesus as the Son of God as well as the Son of Man.[28] In this song, Masilamani draws heavily from Paul's letter to the Colossians in 1:15–20 and highlights the universal lordship of Jesus Christ. In the bhakti tradition, worshippers had their most favored god and occasionally swapped their gods according to the seasons in life. But they seldom juxtaposed gods in competition and claimed one to be the only avatar of the Ultimate Reality. Finding themselves in a context of social conflict and perpetual marginalization, Telugu Christians may have eagerly embraced the missionary claims of the finality of Christ. In the context of multiple and competing claims for divine avatars and in an attempt to highlight the monotheistic view of God, Telugu preachers and Western missionaries among Telugus often ignored the traditional Trinitarian understanding of God, a theological stance Pentecostals helped other Telugu Christians recover.

The belief in the universal lordship and uniqueness of Christ often motivates the missionary consciousness of Telugu Christians. The highest number of hymns in the Telugu hymnal praise and adore Christ, while the second-largest center on the church's missionary obligation. Telugu Christians construe mission as preaching about Christ and inviting people to faith in him. In his song "Dhevuni Varasalamu," Masilamani understands Christians as those on the mission of preaching Christ. Using a military tune and vocabulary, Masilamani calls the singer to lift Jesus's cross as the banner. Masilamani encourages the singer to envision a new world and thus overcome fear and hostility. The song hints both at the social stigma Telugu Christians lived with and at their

---

27  *Andhra Chraistava Keertanalu,* 114.
28  Mark 8:29, 31, 38. Cf. Matt 11:27 and Luke 22:29. The title "Son of God" is used numerous times in the Gospel according to Saint John.

missionary zeal. Masilamani's hymn "Randi Suvartha Sundhamo" is another example of this missionary enthusiasm:

*Come to the presence of gracious Jesus*
*With the melodies of the gospel*
*With amazing songs of the cross*
*With the music of cymbals and sitar*

*Only Jesus is the destiny of humanity*
*Only Jesus is the location for human righteousness*
*Only Jesus is the sanctifying name*
*Jesus shines as the holy name for Christians*

*Only Jesus is the image of divine love*
*Only Jesus is the reflection of omnipresent God*
*Only Jesus is the lord of the people*
*Only Jesus is the safe haven for the poor*

*Only Jesus carried the cross*
*Only Jesus gives eternal life*
*Only Jesus has the authority to forgive*
*Jesus helps those who pray*

*Only Jesus is the illuminator in the church*
*Only Jesus is the only peace within a soul*
*Only Jesus is the living light within a family*
*Jesus blesses the innocent children*

*Only Jesus is the way to heaven*
*Only Jesus is the heaven on earth for worshippers*
*Only Jesus is the strategy for world peace*
*Jesus is the sure hope for humanity.*[29]

---

29 *Andhra Chraistava Keertanalu*, 141.

The song reminds the singer to worship and preach the gospel because Jesus is the only way to God. It is an invitation to the listener to have faith in Christ. Within the religiously pluralist context of India, worship is a site and moment of witness. It is more so because Dalits worship in streets and sanctuaries with loudspeakers. Every song and sermon is an invitation.

Reminiscent of the Hindu bhakti songs, the posture of submission runs through most of Masilamani's hymns. A devotee finds themselves helpless even to follow God. Recognizing the need for grace, the devotee completely submits to the deity. Masilamani accentuates this attitude of submission. According to his most popular song, "Margam chupumu intiki," which reinterprets the parable of the prodigal son (Luke 15:11–32), the worshipper is a rebel in need of God's help to turn to God:

> *Show me the way home to my father's house*
> *Show me the sweet world of love to my eyes (twice)*
>
> *To me who wandered with love for sin, a famine struck*
> *Grant me wholeness as I repent and seek father's blessing*
> *For me who does not deserve to face you*
> *Lord, your cross instilled confidence*
> *Show me the way home . . .*
>
> *Considering wealth as everything and worldly pleasure as heavenly*
> *I have left father for the worldly delights to ruin my life*
> *God, I return to you begging with folded hands*
> *Show me the way*
> *Show me the way home . . .*
>
> *Hoping that life would be better in far off lands, I lost the way*
> *All friends I trusted deserted me, impoverished I am*
> *Pour out your grace on me, Gracious God*

*Deem me blessed*
*Show me the way home . . .*

*With the sting of hunger, I have sold my sense of shame*
*Gutted I am having been ostracized even by pigs*
*Habituated to grief, I reached the ebbs of wickedness*
*Grant me shelter, as the humanity within awakens*
*Show me the way home . . .*

*Complaining that I am not your son and the house a prison, I left*
*Be merciful as I beg to work as one of your slaves*
*Do not turn me away as I have none else to go to*
*Receive me with forgiveness*
*Show me the way home . . .*

*My father saw me, came running, embraced me, and wept*
*He gave me new life, took me home, and blessed me*
*My life story will be a witness to Jesus' love in this world*
*Show me the way home . . .*[30]

In this song written both to retell a biblical story and to invite the listener to faith in God, Masilamani highlights the reality of evil and the need for God's grace. The wayward son repents and returns to God with folded hands, a gesture symbolizing total submission to the deity. The song reminds the singer that God shows the way, grants new life, and welcomes the lost individual back. In addition to bringing Dalits closer to their neighbor Hindus, the posture of submission also reinforces the latter's hierarchal values.

As mentioned earlier, almost all hymns composed by Masilamani are hewn from biblical passages. They retell events in the life of Jesus and highlight the redemptive power of Jesus's death

---

30  *Andhra Chraistava Keertanalu,* 562–653.

and resurrection. For example, Masilamani's song "Andhala Thara Arudhinche Nake" (The blessed star that descended for me) relates the journeys of magi and shepherds to find solace and satisfy their spiritual yearnings at the feet of baby Jesus.

The song "Basillenu Siluvalo Papa Kshema" (At the cross our sins are forgiven) narrates the passion story. Masilamani's leadership in the Bible Society of India as auxiliary secretary for the region of Andhra Pradesh attests to his faith that when retold, the Scriptures are capable of transforming individuals. It also reflects the general Telugu Christian's attitude about the Bible. Accustomed to transmitting the truth in oral stories, Dalit Christians, in imitation of and/or competition with Hindus, embraced Christian Scriptures and found their retelling transforming and empowering.

In conversion to Christianity, Telugu Christians of Dalit and "caste" backgrounds alike abandoned the notion of multiple gods or goddesses in favor of singular allegiance to the lone God revealed in Jesus. The notion of a God who is capable of both suffering and overcoming pain was novel to those of Hindu background but was familiar to those of Dalit descent. Given their sufferings, they found the cross to be the high point in the history of salvation. With their belief in Jesus as the only way to God, Telugu Baptists construed inviting others to faith in Christ as their mission. They viewed unquestioning submission to Christ as central and indispensable to one's discipleship. By emphasizing the spirituality of submission, the dominant caste Christians undermined the spirituality of protest latent in the Dalit religiosity. Subbamma sought to bring into the church the Ashram ethos, which ultimately reinforced a hierarchy within the church, with that of a guru at the top of the hierarchy and followers ranked lower. We shall consider more of these attempts in the following chapter.

# 7

# The Movements around and outside the Church

In an earlier chapter, I narrated the story of Telugu Pentecostals, whose beginnings date back to the 1930s but who had as a movement flourished after the emergence of the state of greater Andhra Pradesh. In the preceding chapter, I have analyzed those efforts in the liturgical churches to intentionally incorporate the local worldviews and integrate them with the traditions from the North Atlantic world. Meanwhile, outside the traditional church structures emerged a few eclectic movements drawing from the Holiness movement of the West and yet challenging the confessional churches. The Laymen's Evangelical Fellowship was founded by Daniel Nagabatthula from Amalapuram.[1] Born a Brethren and consistent with his theological roots, his movement was critical of clergy and promoted personal piety among its followers. Daniel prescribed annual retreats and daily prayers for the members to grow in holiness.[2] Unlike his Pentecostal counterparts, he elevated the gift of prophecy over glossolalia. Among these Holiness movements, I will now discuss the histories and theologies of the Hebron Assemblies (founded by Bakht Singh Chabra, a lay Christian)

---

1 Whitson Paul, "The Laymen's Evangelical Fellowship: An Indigenous Christian Movement in India," in Hedlund, *Christianity Is Indian*, 413.
2 Paul, 414.

and the Bible Mission (pioneered by Devadas Mungamuri, a Lutheran lay leader).

Although it began elsewhere much earlier, the Hebron Assemblies flourished among the Telugus during the second half of the twentieth century. The assemblies were founded by a non-Telugu but embraced by Telugus, as both the founder and his teachings found home in Hyderabad. As a movement centered on an individual, it disintegrated after his death in 2000.

In her comprehensive analysis of the phenomenon, Evangeline Bharathi Nuthalapati locates the origins of the movement in the colonial context and its flourishing to independent India. She traces the beginnings of the movement to the disenchanted Christians within the Anglican churches and the influx of "rational" teachings therein as well as the "anti-colonial struggles."[3] Singh, through his anticlerical sentiments, provided a voice to these disillusioned Christians.

Born in 1903 in Punjab, now located in Pakistan, Singh was a practicing Hindu. Having studied in a mission school, he was familiar with Christianity but was critical of it. Singh grew weary of it because of the laxity of Christians he encountered while studying in England in 1926. During his visits to Canada in 1928 and the following year, Singh came in contact with a group of Christians affiliated with the Christian and Missionary Alliance whose display of piety impressed him.[4] On his return to Canada, Singh became friends with John and Edith Hayword. They introduced him to their brand of Christianity, finally resulting in his conversion in 1933. Upon his return, Singh traveled across the Indian subcontinent, preaching his faith in churches and denouncing the clergy lifestyle. He had visited Hyderabad, a city that later became

---

3  Nuthalapati, *Brother Bakht Singh*, 23.
4  Hedlund, *Christianity Is Indian*, 340.

his home, for the first time in 1939. In his sermons, he criticized the professional clergy for their self-indulgence and lack
of care for their parishioners.[5] Christians disenchanted with
liturgical traditions and the clergy found an appealing haven
in his "fellowship."

Nuthalapati finds imprints of Hindu piety, especially that of
bhakti tradition, on the teachings and practices of the Hebron
Assemblies.[6] She identifies at least three such marks. First, those
in the assemblies deem their understanding of the Scriptures as
the source of authority (*pramanas*).[7] They center their lives on the
voice of God they discern in the Bible. This they posit as a contrast to the confessional traditions that interpret the Scriptures
in the prisms of historical confessions. To endear its members,
the assemblies, also called fellowships, cherry-pick Bible verses
that are comforting or appealing and distribute them to its
members. In essence, the pastoral needs of individuals determine how the Scriptures are viewed and interpreted. Although
these verses were addressed to a different audience and ought to
be interpreted only in the totality of the gospel and their contexts,
the members claim these verses as God's "promises" in their
personal lives.[8] Second, they value their encounters (*anubhav*)
with God and the perpetual experience of being in fellowship with God as central to their devotion.[9] The experience of
being in fellowship with God manifests itself in their relationships with others in the assemblies. Third, in their interpretation of the Scriptures, they address the emotional needs of the
audience.[10] The practices of sitting on the floor, entering the meeting place without shoes, singing local tunes, and adapting local

---

5  Nuthalapati, *Brother Bakht Singh*, 23.
6  Nuthalapati, 36.
7  Nuthalapati, 142.
8  Nuthalapati, 192.
9  Nuthalapati, 85.
10  Nuthalapati, 149.

architecture in building meeting spaces only attest to their affinity with the Hindu cultures.[11]

The Hebron movement was singularly countercultural in its relation to castes.[12] The practice of weekly dinners (love feasts) in which "believers" of all castes gathered and volunteers of any caste served openly challenged the caste distinctions both in the society and in some churches. These local "love feasts" culminated annually in two-and-a-half-week-long "holy convocations" at the state levels. And occasionally, the holy convocations led to the starting of new local assemblies. At the ritual level, the weekly breaking of bread had supported this egalitarian ethos. This practice, which they considered an ordinance, was open to all, provided the participants approached it worthily. One's worthiness to approach the table was measured by continuous repentance and incessant self-examination of one's lifestyle, not by one's birth.[13] The custom of universal kneeling while praying symbolically equalized members of all castes and genders.

The local "fellowships" often consisted of "believers" of all castes, a phenomenon that was atypical of churches founded during the colonial period.[14] The prohibition against being yoked with outsiders, which emerged out of their emphasis on separation from the world, encouraged marriages within the assemblies, often resulting in ecclesiastical endogamy and therefore intercaste marriages. Thus, though they may not have been aware of Bhimrao Ramji Ambedkar's prescriptions to the annihilation of the caste system in Indian society, those in the Hebron Assemblies inadvertently practiced both intercaste dining and intercaste marriage.

---

11 Nuthalapati, 36.
12 Hedlund, *Christianity Is Indian*, 152.
13 Hedlund, 321.
14 Nuthalapati, *Brother Bakht Singh*, 192.

Claiming to be modeled after the NTC, the Hebron movement construed the church as a gathering of believers.[15] They gathered together to worship, study the Bible, observe ordinances, kneel in prayer, and enjoy "love feasts." They considered the rituals of baptism and the Lord's Table as divinely ordained and as practices that any member could officiate, a clear departure from and challenge to the liturgical churches.[16] The care among members extended beyond their gathered moments in prayers for one another. These groups, however, refused to identify themselves as churches but called themselves assemblies or fellowships or gatherings. It may be because of the association of the word *church* with professional clergy and the responsibilities of the members in self-governance. However, these fellowships recognized elders to have been divinely ordained to interpret the Scriptures, administer the ordinances, and govern in the matters of church discipline. When in doubt and conflict, fellowships mostly splintered, as there was no source of authority beyond themselves and no property to lay claim to.[17] These ambivalent attitudes about autonomy and authority problematized their claims to be nondenominational. Drawing resources from the restoration traditions in North America and Europe as well as the bhakti traditions, the Hebron movement provided alternative avenues to those disenchanted with the dominant traditions within the Telugu Church.

## The Bible Mission

The Bible Mission, founded by Devadas, is another movement that drew heavily from the indigenous resources even while retaining some of its Lutheran patterns. Like Hebron, it

---

15 Nuthalapati, 44.

16 Hedlund, *Christianity Is Indian*, 339.

17 Hedlund, 339.

refused to identify itself as a church. Both emerged during the colonial period but flourished in independent India. As mentioned earlier, Nuthalapati identifies the bhakti tradition as a significant contributor to the Hebron Assemblies. Solomon Raj Pulidindi, who has studied the movement in his doctoral dissertation, characterizes the Bible Mission as an indigenous tradition. He cites five reasons it could be classified as indigenous: (1) it was founded by an Indian; (2) its beliefs emerged at the grassroots, as against those from synods and summits; (3) its faith was articulated and communicated in oral traditions, not in written confessions; (4) like folk traditions in the region, the movement celebrated prayers, healing, dreams, visions, and myths; and (5) its structures were less rigid and allowed for individual choices.[18]

As Singh was to the Hebron assemblies, Devadas was the founder and ideologue for the Bible Mission. Devadas's sermons and writings continue to guide the theological trajectory of the movement. The ideological moorings for the movement can be found in several pamphlets, including (1) *Mithra* (A friend), a compendium on the plan of salvation; (2) *Praising the Divine Attributes*, a manual for worship; and (3) *Maxims to Rebuke to Satan*, an anthology in exorcism.[19] These writings are available in audio format so that they can be accessible to everyone, both literate and illiterate. Local preachers add to the freedom and dynamism through their interpretations. At least nine hymns that Devadas wrote found their place in *Andhra Chraistava Keertanalu* and thereby in the faith of Telugu Christians. Two of them—"Deva samsthuti cheyave manasa," a reinterpretation of Psalm 103, and "Thanuvu Nadhidhigo

---

18  Solomon Raj Pulidindi, *A Christian Folk-Religion in India: A Study of the Small Church Movement in Andhra Pradesh, with Special Reference to the Bible Mission of Devadas* (New York: Peter Lang, 1982), 17.

19  Roger Hedlund, *Quest for Identity: India's Churches of Indigenous Origin: The "Little Traditions" in Indian Christianity* (New Delhi: ISPCK, 2000), 103.

ghaikonumi"—continue to be popular in liturgical churches. While the first is sung as an opening hymn, the latter is in response to the sermon. Devadas's hymns continue to catechize Christians both within his movement and beyond.

Born in Jegurupadu to Jonah Mungamuri and his wife, Satyavath, Devadas grew up as a Lutheran in the 1870s.[20] After his high school and subsequent catechist training, Devadas was employed at his alma mater, located on the outskirts of Rajah-mundry, as a teacher, dormitory warden, and instructor.[21] The completion of third forum, an equivalent of eighth grade, was considered sufficient for someone to teach in a school. Although well versed in the Christian Scriptures, respected among peers for his gifts in teaching, and encouraged to pursue ordained ministry, Devadas chose to remain a lay catechist.

Two remarkable events may have changed the trajectory of his vocation and theological fidelity to Lutheran tradition. First, according to Solomon Raj, Devadas met Sadhu Sun-dar Singh and translated the latter's sermon during his visit to Rajahmundry in the 1920s.[22] It is difficult to assess the impact of this encounter between the two except to say that Devadas was so impressed with Singh, he likened himself to Singh in his later life.[23] Both were ascetics, having remained single. Second, Devadas met with Samuel, a Pentecostal preacher, in 1934 during the embryonic stages of Telugu Pentecostalism.[24] Itiner-ant Pentecostal preachers initially reached out to the Christians in confessional churches and sought to convince the latter of the validity of their teachings. Devadas's teachings on spiritual

---

20  There are conflicting claims on the year of his birth, and neither of the claims is supported by documentary evidence. Pulidindi, *Christian Folk Religion*, 42. Cf. Rayi, *Telugulo Chraistava Sahityam*, 80.

21  Pulidindi, *Christian Folk Religion*, 181.

22  Pulidindi, *New Wine-Skins*, 6.

23  Pulidindi, *Christian Folk Religion*, 57.

24  Bergunder, *South Indian Pentecostal Movement*, 113.

baptism resonate with those of Pentecostals. Devadas ranked Samuel as a "prophet like Moses," although we do not know the reasons for the comparison.[25]

The meetings with Singh and Samuel may have significantly contributed to the formation of Devadas's theology and his weaning away from the Lutheran community. We cannot ignore the seeds of disenchantment that date beyond these meetings. When encouraged to seek ordination, Devadas was believed to have claimed to have been ordained by the Spirit as early as 1919, a year before meeting Singh. It is also possible that these inklings of disillusionment motivated him to listen to non-Lutheran itinerant preachers. The ripples of dissatisfaction culminated in a dream in which Devadas saw the words "the Bible Mission" in early 1938. In less than a year, he found allies and foes within his denomination and founded the Bible Mission.[26] Devadas thereafter traversed the Telugu regions, gathered groups, and appointed ministers. He trained pastors in the Bible Mission for decades before he died in a benefactor's house in Kakani in 1960.

Even while retaining the traditional clergy vestments, liturgical practices, and imprints of its birth tradition, the Bible Mission distinguishes itself from Lutheranism in four key beliefs. First, it names itself after the Bible and claims its divine origins. It accuses Lutherans and Wesleyans of being named after human leaders.

Second, by naming the movement after the Bible, Devadas challenged the confessional statements from Europe. His followers believe that doctrines divide but the celebration of the gifts of the Spirit unites.[27]

Third, Devadas was critical of the "mission churches" for their stagnant structures and envisioned the Bible Mission to

25  Pulidindi, *Christian Folk Religion*, 48.

26  Pulidindi, 42.

27  Pulidindi, 46–47.

be a dynamic missionary movement. His followers worship in house churches, more than one in each village or township. Patterned after the first-century churches, the worship is led by the host or the hostess with little or no participation from the members either in worship or in decision-making. Worshippers for the most part are more guests than members. In their refusal to be a covenant community, members neither demand accountability from the preachers nor commit to others except through the "thanksgiving" offerings. In principle, the Bible Mission does not dislocate Christians from their faith communities, but it rather seeks to create a spiritual bond between them.

Fourth, the accent on the Holy Spirit is another pronounced, distinguishing marker. This emphasis manifests itself in several of the mission's paradigms and practices defined by K. Vijayaratnam, an ideologue, and listed by Solomon Raj:[28]

(1) The Spirit can directly anoint and ordain men and women for ministry. She does not need the mediation of the faith community in calling and using individuals for her activity. As noted earlier, Devadas himself claimed to have been called and ordained by the Spirit.

(2) The Holy Spirit bestows some with the power to heal and others with healing—that is, recovery or relief from a sickness without human intervention is not a relic of the past. To facilitate the continued work of the Spirit in healing, those endowed with this gift erect shrines of healing and conduct day-long mass healing rituals.[29] Given their emphasis on the Spirit and the offer of healing regardless of

28 Pulidindi, 50–51. K. Vijayaratnam, one of the founding members of the Bible Mission, later parted ways with Devadas Mungamuri and founded the Church of God of Prophecy in 1958.

29 Pulidindi, 55.

religion, these healing tabernacles (*swasthatha shaa-las*) draw people of all faiths.[30]

(3) Spirits—benevolent and malevolent—exist and move with freedom. The Holy Spirit empowers the believers to connect with and, if needed, negotiate with the spirit world. Through prayers, malevolent spirits can be exorcised.

(4) Congruent with the Dalit understanding of the ancestors, the Bible Mission believes in and invokes the intervention of the ancestral spirits in the people's personal and worship lives. Those gathered for worship await and acknowledge the spiritual presence of Devadas as well as those of other saints. They place an empty chair in the gathering or in solitude to welcome and host saintly spirits that join them in prayer.[31]

(5) The practice of *sannidhi* (presence), awaiting God's countenance in a set-aside time and space, establishes the contact of the living with the Spirit and the ancestors.[32] One can seek and find an "audience with God" in groups—small and big—or solitude.[33]

(6) The Spirit reveals herself not only through the proclamation and interpretation of the Scriptures but also through dreams and visions.[34] This belief in the direct and continuous revelation of God to God's people undermines the role of church councils and preachers who seek to play mediators between human beings and the Spirit.

---

30  Pulidindi, 82.
31  Hedlund, *Quest for Identity*, 76.
32  Pulidindi, *New Wine-Skins*, 7. See also Pulidindi, *Christian Folk Religion*, 57.
33  Pulidindi, *Christian Folk Religion*, 198.
34  Pulidindi, 86.

(7) Like their Pentecostal counterparts, most of the people of the Bible Mission believe in glossolalia.[35]

With its emphasis on the Spirit, affinity with folk traditions, and distance from imported doctrines, the Bible Mission established a movement beyond the traditional church structures but yet identified itself with the Bible and Christ.

## The Movements beyond the Church

In addition to the Holiness movements that drew extensively from the indigenous worldviews and expressly identified themselves as Christian, the second half of the nineteenth century had also seen movements that explicitly refused to identify themselves as Christian. These have been critical of the practices of baptism and the Lord's Table. The ideology proposed by Venkata Chalam Gudipati (1894–1979) illustrates such an encounter. Chalam, a Telugu philosopher, initially identified himself as a rationalist.

A Brahmin, Chalam grew up in a Hindu family well versed in Hindu scriptures. A prolific writer, he joined a guild of writers and resided in Rajahmundry. Having been introduced to Christian missionaries through his wife in Eluru, he admired their critical attitudes toward the local traditions.[36] Once a fierce critic of the Hindu traditions, he eventually evolved an ideologically eclectic movement that incorporated elements from the worldviews he had previously challenged. He gathered a messianic community and propagated an apocalyptic inbreaking in history when the Lord would establish an egalitarian society.[37] After he died in 1974, his daughter, Souris Pramoda (also known as Maatha Souris or Maharshi Souris), inherited the

---

35  Pulidindi, 50–51.
36  Sudharshanam, *Chalam*, 31.
37  Sudharshanam, 49.

ashram in Bheemunipatnam, where the residents and visitors await an apocalyptic end to the present era, a concept latent with Christianity. The nineteenth-century Raja Yogi tradition, founded by Potuluri Veerabrahmam, had earlier appropriated this teaching.

In his writings, Chalam comments extensively on the teachings of Jesus. In his novel *Martha*, he summarizes the life of Jesus. The choice of the title of the book itself emphasizes the role women played in the life of Jesus. In this fictional conversation centered on events in John 11, Chalam uses the words of Martha and Mary Magdalene to portray his understanding of Jesus. Chalam understands Jesus as *sampurna manavudu*— that is, as a perfect human being and who thus can be considered *Ishvara puthrudu* (the Son of God). Four facets of Jesus reveal his wholeness: Jesus (1) identified himself with the poor, (2) challenged those in power, (3) healed the sick, and (4) exorcised demonic spirits. An advocate of women's equality, Chalam presents Jesus as the one who not only respected women but had also charged them to lead his disciples after his death. Resonant with and reminiscing her father's beliefs, Pramoda considers Jesus Christ as a *jnani* (wise man) and challenges the church's claims over Christ.[38]

### Subba Rao Kalagara's *Sampradhaya* (Tradition)

The encounter between the local worldviews and Christianity took another shape and, like Chalam's, located itself outside the church in the *sampradhaya* (practice) founded by Subba Rao Kalagara. Even though he deeply loved and ardently followed Christ, Subba Rao refused to call himself a Christian. He

---

38 A YouTube interview conducted by A. B. Anand with Souris Pramoda: "'Souris' Chalam (Writer) Daughter Interview," A. B. Anand, November 10, 2018, YouTube video, 1:04:51, https://www.youtube.com/watch?v=0rqsI08J5KI.

preferred Christ to Christianity as an institution. Kaj Baago, a church historian, characterizes Subba Rao's teachings as a Hindu response to Christ.[39] K. P. Aleaz construes the movement as an embodiment of the gospel in the terms of Advaita Vedanta and calls it "an authentic Hindu-Christian" encounter.[40] Richard L. Hivner understands the *sampradhaya* as an eclectic movement.[41]

We do not know much about the life of Subba Rao except through the autobiographical account he provided to Baago and to one of his followers, Daniel C. Airan, late in his life.[42] According to it, Subba Rao was born in Eluru in 1912 and moved to Kolkata in his teens, where he completed his college education.[43] He then moved to Mysore and completed another degree in education. After his studies, Subba Rao returned home to the Krishna district and was appointed as a headmaster in Pamarru in a school administered by the British colonial school board.[44] At the age of thirty-one, Subba Rao received what he called a divine vision, an experience associated with his illness.[45] After receiving this extraordinary dream, he realized that he not only received healing but also was given the power to heal sicknesses and exorcise malevolent spirits in the name of Jesus.

Subba Rao began to read the Christian Scriptures but was reluctant to publicly admit his admiration for Christ. He

---

39  Kaj Baago, *The Movement around Subba Rao: A Study of the Hindu-Christian Movement around K. Subba Rao in Andhra Pradesh* (Madras, India: CLS, 1968), 2.

40  K. P. Aleaz, *Christian Thought through Advaita Vedanta*, Contextual Theological Education Series (Delhi: ISPCK, 1996), 41.

41  Richard L. Hivner, *Exploring the Depths of the Mystery of Christ: K. Subba Rao's Eclectic Praxis of Hindu Discipleship to Jesus* (Bangalore, India: Center for Contemporary Christianity, 2005).

42  Baago, *Subba Rao*.

43  Baago. See also Aleaz, *Christian Thought*, 41.

44  Pulidindi, *Christian Folk Religion*, 3.

45  Hivner, *Exploring the Depths*, 45–46.

remained an anonymous follower, perhaps because of the stigma attached to Christianity, until his wife, Nagendramma, fell ill and, during her hallucinations, began to recite biblical verses. He was startled and then eventually gathered courage after her recovery to confess his admiration for Christ and the Bible. He teamed up with his wife to share his fascination for Christ with his community members. He composed thirty-four songs both to express his love for Jesus and to promote this *sampradhaya*.[46] In these songs, he extolled Jesus as *satguru* (true teacher / teacher of truth).[47] He interpreted Jesus's teachings but refused to limit them to a religious system. Considering Jesus as his religion, ritual, ideology, and life destination, he refused to substitute the latter to Jesus.

Seeing himself as a relentless critic of institutional religion, Subba Rao denounced the Christian communities, especially their clergy and rituals. After his conversion, he claimed to have met church leaders, especially those of Lutheran and Baptist backgrounds, in the region with competing claims to the truth of the gospel. He refused to join any. He similarly rejected baptism, considered to be a sacrament by some and ordinance by others but a rite of initiation to almost all of them. He wondered, If the waters had the power to cleanse humans from sins, why would God send God's begotten son to be killed for human redemption?

Like Chalam, Subba Rao considered Jesus as the one who has mastered the *jnana* (wisdom)—one of the three paths, with *karma* (benevolence) and *bhakti* (devotion) as the other two—to *moksha* (liberation). Deeming *jnana* as liberation, Subba Rao saw no need for sacraments, which Christians considered the means of grace. He viewed the beliefs about and practices of sacraments as superstitious and thus antithetical to the *jnana* Jesus

46 Hivner compiled the translations of these songs, which have been translated by Solomon Raj Pulidindi and corroborated by me.
47 Aleaz, *Christian Thought*, 43.

had taught. Sacraments, according to him, emerged out of and contributed to *ajnana* (foolishness).[48] He believed that Jesus taught the truth to set humans free but that the church teaches foolishness to hold Jesus and people captive to its superstitions.

Positing the traditional church directly as antithetical, Subba Rao gathered a group of followers. He introduced no ritual of initiation but ritualized weekly gatherings.[49] He, however, was hesitant to call these gathered moments worship services, as Christ demanded discipleship but not shallow obeisance. These weekly gatherings focused on reading the teachings of Christ and seeking healing from ailments through prayer. Subba Rao's followers met in large halls within or adjacent to their houses. Belonging to the landowning and thereby affluent families, their residences could accommodate groups of people. Given the number of people gathering, Subba Rao himself added a hall to his house that could accommodate approximately a hundred people.[50] During the meetings, those present read a text from the New Testament, followed by a brief exposition from a leader. Subba Rao himself interpreted when he was alive, and his wife, Nagendramma, continued after his death. Baago, who visited the worship site in the late 1960s, recalled that the singing of the lyrics composed by Subba Rao followed and often resulted in ecstasy.[51] These gatherings ended with prayers for the divine intervention in the personal crises of those attending, culminating in a holy meal, a ritual in itself. People in crises traveled to his house throughout the week to seek his prayers. He never guaranteed to heal, nor did he claim that he could. Subba Rao reminded his clients that those who were destined (karma)

---

48  Baago, *Subba Rao*, 13.
49  Baago.
50  I personally visited the place in 2005, when Subba Rao's widow, Nagen-dramma, was active.
51  Baago, *Subba Rao*, 8.

would be healed.[52] Crowds, drawn mostly from the landowning Kamma community, gathered not only in the district but also in Vijayawada and Hyderabad. Subba Rao had traveled widely in other states of the country, appointed leaders in each gathered group, and thus institutionalized the movement.

These gatherings continued when I last visited the center in the summer of 2005. Those in need of relief and recovery continue to flock. Subba Rao's tomb stands at the center of the meeting place and is believed to mediate the healing energy. Many folk traditions both within and across religious traditions venerate tombs as sacred spaces and abodes of healing. The popular *dargahs* (tombs) of Muslim saints draw multitudes and are considered places of healing.[53]

In the progression of thought and the complexities thereof, Subba Rao's hostility toward the local Christian communities did not waver. Before he followed Christ in 1942, he viewed and detested Christ as the "God of untouchables."[54] This impression may have arisen because of the group conversions of Dalits to Christianity. Since the church was identified with the Dalits, it was stigmatizing for any non-Dalit to join the established churches.[55] Given his social location as a landowning, literate, and affluent Kamma, this belief and the very practice of baptism may have been problematic. Subba Rao compared the rite of baptism, in which those baptized were believed to have been cleansed, with that of washing dirty pigs. Subba Rao preached that waters do not purify, but the Christ experience does.[56]

---

52  Pulidindi, *Christian Folk Religion*, 5.

53  Joyce Burkhalter Flueckiger's book *In Amma's Healing Room: Gender and Vernacular Islam in South Asia* (Bloomington: Indiana University Press, 2006) is an exceptional commentary on one of such sacred sites.

54  Baago, *Subba Rao*, 8.

55  Baago, 8.

56  Goshing, *Christian*, 436.

The sight of Dalit pastors, whom the landowning castes despised, and their claims to sanctity would have been infuriating to any Kamma with claims to a divine vision. In one of his songs, Subba Rao describes the clergy as those engaged in ministry to gratify their bellies. Subba Rao was critical of all godmen, but the references to the Christian clergy allude to poverty and the greed it generates. The questions of social location and changed political environments and their impact on one's response to Christ help us understand these movements. With his association of the church with Dalits and dexterous rendering of the Christian message in Advaitic terms, Subba Rao opened up ideological space outside the church for those of the landowning Kammas who would not otherwise follow Christ. These traditions within, around, and outside the church skillfully and imaginatively brought together evangelical values and local cultures, both folk and bhakti.

# 8

# Conclusion

The numbers have increased from ten million to twenty-four million in 2001,[1] but this does not reflect the percentages of Christians in the overall population of independent India. It remains 2.3 percent.[2] The number of Telugu Christians in 1961 was 1,428,729 and decreased to 1,181,917.[3] But the numbers do not tell the whole story. They do not tell the story of Telugu Christians in the new millennium. Telugu Christians shaped the Telugu cultures, and they have also been shaped by it. In this book, I narrated the history of Telugu Christians, with a special focus on the appropriation of the Christian message among the Telugus and the diverse interest groups behind it.

As you may have noticed, I did not analyze the diverse social agendas and political interests of the missionaries but rather on the local Christians.

Christians from the landowning Sudhras communities, the beneficiaries of the caste system, and those of Brahmins origins have made an indelible mark on the reception and transmission of Christianity. Their facility with letters and their access to the pulpit provided them opportunities to Sanskritize

---

1  "The First Report on Religion Data," Census of India 2001, http://lsi
   .gov.in:8081/jspui/bitstream/123456789/60/1/41020_2001_REL.pdf.
2  "Population Growth and Religious Composition," Pew Research Center,
   September 21, 2021, https://www.pewforum.org/2021/09/21/population
   -growth-and-religious-composition/.
3  "The First Report on Religion Data."

Christianity. Most Telugu Christians live in the rural areas, and the nature of their relationships therein facilitated the process of Sanskritization.

When pushed to the social margins, the disenfranchised groups, especially the Dalits, used belief systems, both local and global, to find meaning in their current plight and negotiate for dignity. The strategies included evolving their worldviews, reinterpreting the dominant traditions, and embracing religious alternatives from elsewhere. Christianity introduced by Catholic and Protestant missionaries provided them an opportunity. In addition to giving them a global outreach, it had also brought them into a new faith community with their erstwhile oppressors. By associating with Christianity, they have untapped the subversive potential of it. However, in their quest for social dignity, Dalit Christians have also emulated some of the Brahminical practices of the dominant castes and the ethos behind those practices.

Custodians and transmitters of their worldviews, Telugu women of both "caste" and Dalit backgrounds have embraced and interpreted Christianity as preachers, schoolteachers, health workers, and writers. Home is a crucial terrain in faith formation, and so is the place of women at home. In their mediating and modeling of the Christian faith and practice, Telugu Christian women, in alliance with their missionary counterparts, have recovered and heightened the holistic and immediate nature of the gospel.

Prompted by their enthusiasm to share their faith, Western—Roman Catholic and Protestant—missionaries traveled to and resided on the Indian subcontinent during the colonial era. They navigated the fluctuating and conflicting political equations and social interests of the European colonizers, local rulers, dominating groups, and social outcasts. Missionaries did not always find the allies they were looking for and could not execute strategies they came with. When demanded by historical contingencies and local dynamics, they altered their strategies and allied with the downtrodden, which they may not have planned to do. Some of them recognized the God of the poor the local Christians had highlighted in the gospel they preached, especially during the era of mass conversions.

In this five-centuries-long complex negotiation between the various interest groups and their sociospiritual aspirations, Dalit Christians and "caste" coreligionists have shared their love of letters. As noted earlier, the facilities to read and write were ancient but were confined to some communities. The schools established by the missionaries and often aided by the colonial rulers opened up opportunities for the groups, especially women and Dalits, to acquire new modes of learning and living as well as nontraditional occupations, thus slightly altering their social status. This emphasis on literacy emerged out of the notion shared among the local Christians and the Western missionaries that Christianity is a religion of the book and undeniably due to the modernity they were ushered into in the period under study.

This religion of the book generated interest not in books in general but in the Bible. Although the interest levels may vary, the love for the Christian Scriptures is shared across the confessional boundaries. Some have learned to read for the sole purpose of reading the Bible. With their love for the Christian Scriptures, Telugu Christians of all confessional shades weave biblical verses and narratives into the songs they sing. They memorize and recite the scriptural portions for both their own edification and that of their congregations. Not only are the Bible sounds and letters sacred, but the Bible as a material artifact is too. The reverence Hindus and Muslims have for their sacred texts reverberates in Telugu Christian attitudes toward the Bible.

Telugu Christians take their calling to verbally share faith, which they construe to be the "truth," with others seriously. With this conceived mandate, they look for opportunities to invite others to have faith in Christ. They have evolved a lifestyle, attire, and dictions that are remarkably distinguishable—at least in the sight of non-Christian Telugus. Their eagerness to profess their faith in public and interpersonal conversations, as long as it does not hurt their professional or business interests, also ought to be seen as a measure of their self-assertion. Sharing one's faith with others in the hopes of welcoming them into one's faith is not alien to the Telugus, as their Buddhist ancestors had done so before the Common Era, and the Hindu and Muslim ancestors did so in the Common Era. Moreover, the Telugu Christian community is a product of the missionary activities of European and North American missionaries, whose goal was the same—to share their faith with others to welcome them into their fold.

As Geoffrey Oddie has astutely and incisively argued, social protest was one of the factors in the massive conversions of Dalits in the second half of the nineteenth and the first half of the twentieth centuries. Political considerations have played a decisive role either in welcoming or in rejecting the Christian faith in the premodern period. Telugus have lived in a religiously sanctioned caste system long enough to recognize the social implications of religion. Telugu Christians have recognized the civil nature of the gospel, at least during the colonial era. As noted in the second half of this volume, otherworldly tendencies erupted in songs and sermons during the postcolonial period and thus quelled the socially subversive nature of their Christian beliefs.

The attempts to undermine the subversive nature of the Christian faith began during the colonial period itself. No doubt the colonial interpretations of the Bible might have contributed to this subservient attitude. I have not studied the hermeneutical plots of the missionaries in this volume, not to absolve them, but to focus my energies on the Telugu Christians. The hymns written by Brahmin Christians and their dominant caste allies and wholeheartedly embraced and internalized by the dominated groups prove to be palpable evidence of how the theme of submission has infiltrated the Telugus' understanding of the gospel. To earn social respect, Dalit Christians swapped their pre-Christian spirituality of resistance with that of submission derived from the bhakti tradition.

Given the history of caste and gender hierarchies, the notion of equality is alien to Telugu culture. This blind spot often plays not only into church governance but also into the theology of the Telugus. The European church polities that Christian missionaries transported have been contextualized by the Telugu Church leader, and almost every governing mechanism resonates with the local feudal culture more than with those of their counterparts abroad. This explains the presence of bishops in congregational or free churches as well as the unequal share of powers among the ecclesiastical offices. When translated into theology, it is inconceivable for a Telugu mind to treat the three persons in the Trinity as equal. This often carries into interpersonal relationships with local Christian communities, especially in terms of caste and gender.

In sum, the power dynamics in the process of the translation of the Christian message and the political interests of the groups involved together produced a faith community that is both avowedly Christian and extremely Sanskritic. The confluence of three worldviews—Christian, Dalit, and Hindu—resulted in a Christian community that confesses Christ, has acquired literacy, reveres the Bible, and is missionary minded, otherworldly, socially disengaged, and hierarchical.

# Selected Bibliography

## Monographs

Adami, Rebecca. *Women and the Universal Declaration of Human Rights.* New York: Routledge, 2020.

Airan, Daniel C. *Kalagara Subba Rao: The Mystic of Munipalle.* Vijayawada, India: privately published by Kutumba Rao, n.d.

———. *The Miracle Man of Munipalle.* Vijayawada, India: Vidyalaya, 1963.

Aleaz, K. P. *Christian Thought through Advaita Vedanta.* Contextual Theological Education Series. Delhi: ISPCK, 1996.

Anderson, Allan. *To the Ends of the Earth: Pentecostalism and the Transformation of World Christianity.* New York: Oxford University Press, 2013.

Archibald, Mabel Evangeline. *Glimpses and Gleams of India and Bolivia: The Jubilee Book of Mission Bands.* Toronto: American Baptist Publication Society for Baptist Women's Missionary Societies of Canada, 1923.

Arles, Siga, and Brian Wintle, eds. *Striving for Excellence: Educational Ministry in the Church.* Bangalore, India: Center for Contemporary Christianity, 2007.

Baago, Kaj. *The Movement around Subba Rao: A Study of the Hindu-Christian Movement around K. Subba Rao in Andhra Pradesh.* Madras, India: CLS, 1968.

Baskerville, Agnes E. *Radiant Lights and Little Candles: Being a Group of Stories of Indian Characters for Children.* N.p., 1985.

Bathineni, Venkata Subbamma. *Christ Confronts India: Indigenous Expression of Christianity in India.* Madras, India: Diocesan, 1973.

Bergunder, Michael. *The South Indian Pentecostal Movement in the Twentieth Century*. Studies in the History of Christian Missions Series. Grand Rapids, MI: Eerdmans, 2008.

Bromley, Eustace B. *They Were Men Sent from God: A Centenary Record (1836–1936) of Gospel Work in India amongst Telugus in the Godavari Delta and Neighbouring Parts*. Bangalore, India: Scripture Literature Press, 1937.

Carman, John B., and Vasantha Rao Chilkuri. *Christians in South India: 1958–2008*. Grand Rapids, MI: Eerdmans, 2014.

Carman, John Spencer. *Rats, Plague, and Religion: Stories of Medical Mission Work in India*. Philadelphia: Judson, 1936.

Chilkuri, Vasantha Rao. *Jathara: A Festival of Christian Witness*. Delhi: ISPCK, 1997.

Chowdhari, John. *Biography of the Rev. Purushottam Chowdhari*. Madras, India: CLS, 1906.

Churchill, Matilda F. *Letters from My Home in India*. Edited and arranged by Grace McLeod Rogers. Toronto: McClelland, Goodchild & Stewart, 1916.

Clarke, Flora. *Sisters: Canada and India*. Moncton, NB: Maritime Press, 1939.

Clough, John. *Social Christianity in the Orient: The Story of a Man, a Mission and a Movement*. New York: Macmillan, 1914.

Correia-Afonsa, John. *Jesuit Letters and Indian History, 1542–1773*. Bombay: Oxford University Press, 1969.

Craig, John. *Forty Years among the Telugus: A History of the Mission of the Baptists of Ontario and Quebec, Canada, to the Telugus, South India, 1867–1907*. Toronto: CBFMB, 1908.

Craig, John, John R. Stillwell, Carrie H. Archibald, and Agnes E. Baskerville, eds. *Telugu Trophies: The Jubilee Story of Some of the Principal Telugu Converts in the Canadian Baptist Foreign Mission in India from 1874 to 1924*. Toronto: CBFMB, 1925.

Cronin, Vicent. *A Pearl to India: The Life of Roberto de Nobili*. New York: E. P. Dutton, 1959.

Daniel, Orville E. *Moving with the Times: The Story of Outreach from Canada into Asia, South America, and Africa*. Toronto: CBFMB, 1973.

Dann, Robert B. *Father of Faith Missions: The Life and Times of Anthony Norris Groves*. London: Authentic Media, 2004.

Davis, John E. *The Life Story of a Leper: Autobiography of John E. Davis*. Toronto: CBFMB, 1918.

Dekar, Paul. *For the Healing of the Nations: Baptist Peacemakers*. Macon, GA: Smyth & Helwys, 1993.

Dolbeer, Martin Luther, R. D. Augustus, and Clarence H. Swavely. *Biographical Record of the Pastors, Missionaries and Prominent Laymen of the United Lutheran Church Mission and the Andhra Evangelical Lutheran Church*. Rajahmundry, India: Silver Jubilee Committee of the AELC, 1955.

Downie, David. *From the Mill to Mission Field: An Autobiography of David Downie*. Philadelphia: Judson, 1928.

Downs, Frederick S. *History of Christianity in India: North East India in the Nineteenth and Twentieth Centuries*. Vol. 5. Pt. 5. Bangalore, India: Church History Association of India, 1992.

Drach, George, and Calvin F. Kuder. *The Telugu Mission of the General Council of the Evangelical Lutheran Church in North America*. Philadelphia: General Council Publication House, 1914.

Elmore, Wilber Theodore. *Dravidian Gods in Modern Hinduism: A Study of the Local and Village Deities of Southern India*. Hamilton, NY: privately published by the author, 1915.

Firth, Cyril Bruce. *An Introduction to Indian Church History*. Madras, India: CLS, 1961.

Fishman, Alvin T. *Culture Change and the Underprivileged: A Study of Madigas in South India under Christian Guidance*. Madras, India: CLS, 1941.

Flueckiger, Joyce Burkhalter. *In Amma's Healing Room: Gender and Vernacular Islam in South Asia*. Bloomington: Indiana University Press, 2006.

Forrester, Duncan N. *Caste and Christianity: Attitudes and Policies on Caste of Anglo-Saxon Protestant Missions in India*. London: Curzon, 1980.

Frykenberg, Robert Eric. *Guntur District, 1788–1848: A History of Local Influence and Central Authority in South India*. Oxford: Clarendon, 1965.

———. *History of Christianity in India: From Beginnings to the Present*. New York: Oxford University Press, 2008.

Fuchs, Stephen. *Rebellious Prophets: A Study of Messianic Movements in Indian Religions*. Bombay: Asia Publishing House, 1965.

George, Bill. *Until All Have Heard*. Cleveland, TN: Church of God World Missions, 2010.

George, K. M. *Church of South India: Life in Union, 1947–1997*. Delhi: ISPCK, 1999.

Gledstone, Frederick F. *The CMS Telugu Mission: Being a Short Account of the Hundred Years 1841–1941*. Mysore, India: Wesley, 1941.

Gnanadason, Joy. *A Forgotten History: The Story of the Missionary Movement and the Liberation of People in South Travancore*. Columbia, MO: South Asia Books, 1996.

Goodall, Norman. *A History of the London Mission Society: 1895–1945*. London: Oxford University Press, 1954.

Grafe, Hugald. *The History of the Work of the Hermannsburg Mission and Evangelical Lutheran Mission (ELM) for the South Andhra Lutheran Church (SALC)*. Chennai, India: Inter-Church Service Association Books, 2010.

Hambye, S. J. *History of Christianity in India: Eighteenth Century*. Vol. 3. Bangalore, India: Church History Association of India, 1997.

Harper, Susan Billington. *In the Shadow of the Mahatma: Bishop V. S. Azariah and the Travails of Christianity in British India*. Grand Rapids, MI: Eerdmans, 2000.

Hedlund, Roger, ed. *Christianity Is Indian: The Emergence of an Indigenous Community*. Delhi: ISPCK, 2000.

————. *Quest for Identity: India's Churches of Indigenous Origin: The "Little Traditions" in Indian Christianity*. Delhi: ISPCK, 2000.

Heras, Henry. *The Aravidu Dynasty of Vijayanagara*. Madras, India: B. G. Paul, 1927.

Hibbert Ware, G. *Christian Missions in the Telugu Country*. London: SPG, 1912.

Hill, Patricia. *The World Their Household: The American Woman's Foreign Mission Movement and Cultural Transformation, 1870–1920*. Ann Arbor: University of Michigan Press, 1985.

Hines, Herbert Waldo. *Clough: Kingdom-Builder in South India*. Philadelphia: Judson, 1929.

Hiney, Tom. *On the Missionary Trail: A Journey through Polynesia, Asia, and Africa with the London Missionary Society*. New York: Atlantic Monthly Press, 2000.

Hivner, Richard L. *Exploring the Depths of the Mystery of Christ: K. Subba Rao's Eclectic Praxis of Hindu Discipleship to Jesus*. Bangalore, India: Center for Contemporary Christianity, 2005.

Hooper, John Stirling Morley, and W. J. Culshaw. *Bible Translations in India, Pakistan and Ceylon*. Bombay: Oxford University Press, 1963.

Jones, Arun. *Missionary Christianity and Local Religion: American Evangelicalism in North India, 1836–1870*. Waco, TX: Baylor University Press, 2017.

Kalagara, Subba Rao. *Gurudev! Where Can I Get So Many Millstones?* Munipalle, India: privately printed by the author, n.d.

————. *Retreat Padre*. Machilipatnam, India: n.p., 1972.

Komanapalli, Rachel Jyothi. *A Man Sent from God: Life Story and Messages of Apostle P. L. Paramjyoti*. Hyderabad, India: Manna Ministries, 2012.

Kooiman, Dick. *Conversion and Social Equality in India: The London Missionary Society in South Travancore in the 19th Century*. New Delhi: Manohar, 1989.

Kroot, Antonius. *History of the Telugu Christians*. Trichinopoly, India: Mill Hill St. Joseph Society, 1910.

Kugler, Anna Sarah. *Guntur Mission Hospital, Guntur, India*. Philadelphia: Women's Missionary Society of the United Lutheran Church in America, 1928.

Leonard, John Greenfield. *Kandukuri Viresalingam (1848–1919): A Biography of an Indian Social Reformer*. Hyderabad, India: Telugu University Press, 1991.

Leoncini, John. *A History of the Catholic Diocese of Vijayawada*. Secunderabad, India: Vani, 1988.

LNR [Ellen Henrietta Ranyard]. *The Missing Link, or Bible-Women in the Homes of the London Poor*. New York: Robert Carter & Brothers, 1860.

————. *Nurses for the Needy or Bible-Women Nurses in the Homes of the London Poor*. London: James Nisbet, 1875.

Luke, P. Y., and John B. Carman. *Village Christians and Hindu Culture*. London: Lutterworth, 1968.

Malik, Yogendra K. *South Asian Intellectuals and Social Change: A Study of the Role of Vernacular-Speaking Intelligentsia*. New Delhi: Heritage, 1982.

Manickam, Sundararaj. *The Social Setting of Christian Conversion in South India: The Impact of the Wesleyan Methodist Missionaries on the Trichy-Tanjore Diocese with Special Reference to the Harijan Communities of the Mass Movement Area, 1820–1947*. Wiesbaden, Germany: Franz Steiner Verlag, 1977.

McGavran, Donald A. *Church Growth: Strategies That Work*. Nashville, TN: Abingdon, 1980.

McLaurin, Mary Stillwell. *25 Years On: 1924–1949*. Toronto: CBFMB, n.d.

Mullens, Joseph. *Missions in South India: Visited and Described*. London: W. H. Dalton, 1854.

Mundadan, Mathias. *History of Christianity in India: From the Beginning up to the Middle of the Sixteenth Century*. Vol. 1. Bangalore, India: Church History Association of India, 1989.

Munson, Arley Isabel. *Jungle Days: Being the Experiences of an American Woman Doctor in India*. New York: Appleton, 1913.

Neill, Stephen Charles. *A History of Christianity in India, 1707–1858*. Vol. 3. Cambridge: Cambridge University Press, 1985.

———. *A History of Christian Missions*. London: Penguin, 1990.

Oddie, Geoffrey, ed. *Religion in South Asia: Religious Conversion and Revival Movements in South Asia in Medieval and Modern Times*. London: Curzon, 1977.

———. *Social Protest in India: British Protestant Missionaries and Social Reforms, 1850–1900*. New Delhi: Manohar, 1979.

Oldfield, Barbara. *Dr. P.J. Titus: God's Man for India*. Bheemunipatnam, India: Church on the Rock, 1996.

Orchard, Malcolm L., and Katherine S. McLaurin. *The Enterprise: The Jubilee Story of the Canadian Baptist Mission in India, 1874–1924*. Toronto: CBFMB, 1925.

Padma, Sree, and A. W. Barber, eds. *Buddhism in the Krishna River Valley of Andhra*. Albany: State University of New York Press, 2008.

Paul, Rajaiah D. *Chosen Vessels: Lives of Ten Indian Christian Pastors of the Eighteenth and Nineteenth Centuries*. Madras, India: CLS, 1961.

———. *Triumphs of His Grace: Lives of Eight Indian Christian Laymen of the Early Days of Protestant Christianity in India, Every One of Whom Was a Triumph of His Grace*. Madras, India: CLS, 1967.

Pickett, Jarrell W. *Christian Mass Movements in India: A Study with Recommendations*. New York: Abingdon, 1933.

Pintchman, Tracy, ed. *Women's Lives, Women's Rituals in the Hindu Tradition*. New York: Oxford University Press, 2007.

Pritchard, John. *Methodists and Their Missionary Societies 1900–1996*. New York: Ashgate, 2014.

Pulidindi, Solomon Raj. *A Christian Folk-Religion in India: A Study of the Small Church Movement in Andhra Pradesh, with Special Reference to the Bible Mission of Devadas*. New York: Peter Lang, 1982.

———. *The New Wine-Skins: The Story of the Indigenous Missions in Coastal Andhra Pradesh, India*. Delhi: ISPCK, 2003.

Rajpramukh, K. E. *Dalit Christians of Andhra: Under the Impact of Missionaries*. New Delhi: Serials, 2008.

Ramakrishna, V. *Social Reform in Andhra: 1848–1919*. New Delhi: Vikas, 1983.

Randall, Ian M., and Anthony R. Cross. *Baptists and Mission: Papers from the Fourth International Conference on Baptist Studies*. Keynes, UK: Paternoster, 2007.

Rapaka, Yabbeju. *Dalit Pentecostalism: A Study of the Indian Pentecostal Church of God, 1932–2000*. Lexington, KY: Emeth, 2013.

Ratnanjali, Sudha. *Purshothama Chowdari Jeevitha Charitra*. Chennai, India: CLS, 1997.

Rauschenbusch-Clough, Emma. *While Sewing Sandals: Tales of a Telugu Pariah Tribe*. New York: Fleming H. Revell, 1899.

Ravela, Joseph. *Bhakti Theology of Purushottam Choudari*. Chennai, India: CLS, 2004.

Rayi, Ratna Sundara Rao. *Bhakti Theology in the Telugu Hymnal*. Madras, India: CLS, 1983.

———. *Telugulo Chraistava Sahityam*. Visakhapatnam, India: Rayi Foundation, 2016.

Robert, Dana. *American Women in Mission: A Social History of Their Theory and Practice*. Macon, GA: Mercer University Press, 1984.

Ross, Andrew. *A Vision Betrayed: The Jesuits in Japan and China, 1542–1742*. Maryknoll, NY: Orbis, 1994.

Rowdon, Harold H. *The Origins of the Brethren, 1825–1850*. London: Pickering & Inglis, 1967.

Sackett, F. Colyer. *Posnett of Medak*. London: Cargate, 1951.

————. *Vision and Venture: A Record of Fifty Years in Hyderabad, 1879–1929.* London: Cargate, 1931.

Sanneh, Lamin. *Translating the Message: The Missionary Impact on Culture.* Maryknoll, NY: Orbis, 1989.

Schmitthenner, Peter. *Telugu Resurgence: C. P. Brown and Cultural Consolidation in Nineteenth-Century South India.* New Delhi: Manohar, 2001.

Sebastian, Joe S. *The Jesuit Carnatic Mission: The Foundation of the Andhra Church.* Secunderabad, India: Jesuit Province Society, 2004.

Sharma, Sripad Ram. *The Religious Policy of the Mughal Emperors.* Bombay: Asia Publishing House, 1972.

Shourie, Arun. *Missionaries in India: Continuities, Changes, and Dilemmas.* New Delhi: HarperCollins, 1998.

Singh, Maina Chawla. *Gender, Religion, and "Heathen Lands": American Missionary Women in South Asia, 1860s–1940s.* New York: Garland, 2000.

Spence, Jonathan D. *The Memory Palace of Matteo Ricci.* London: Penguin, 1985.

Srinivas, M. N. *Social Change in Modern India.* Los Angeles: University of California Press, 1967.

Stanton, William Arthur. *The Awakening of India: Forty Years among the Telugus.* Portland: Falmouth, 1950.

————. *Out of the East: India's Search for God.* New York: Fleming H. Revell, 1938.

Stunt, William T. *Turning the World Upside Down: A Century of Missionary Endeavour.* Bath, UK: Echoes of Service, 1972.

Sundkler, Bengt. *Church of South India: The Movement towards Union, 1900–1947.* London: Lutterworth, 1965.

Swavely, Clarence H., ed. *One Hundred Years in the Andhra Country: A History of the India Mission of the United Lutheran Church in America.* Madras, India: Diocesan, 1942.

Taneti, James Elisha. *Caste, Gender, and Christianity in Colonial India: Telugu Women in Mission*. New York: Palgrave Macmillan, 2013.

———. *History of the Telugu Christians: An Annotated Bibliography*. Lanham, MD: Scarecrow Press, 2011.

Tatford, Frederick A. *The Challenge of India: That the World May Believe*. Vol. 5. Bath, UK: Echoes of Service, 1984.

Thanugundla, Solomon. *Structures of the Church in Andhra Pradesh: An Historico-Juridical Study*. Secunderabad, India: Karuna Sri, 1977.

Thekkedath, Joseph. *History of Christianity in India: From the Middle of the Sixteenth to the End of the Seventeenth Century, 1542–1700*. Vol. 2. Bangalore, India: Church History Association of India, 1982.

Thomas, Parumootil Joseph. *100 Indian Witnesses to Jesus Christ*. Bombay: Bombay Tract and Book Society, 1974.

Thomas, Varghese V. *Dalit Pentecostalism: Spirituality of the Empowered Poor*. Bangalore, India: Asian Trading Corporation, 2008.

Thurston, Edgar. *Castes and Tribes of Southern India*. Vol. 4. Madras, India: Government Press, 1909.

Timpany, Americus V. *The Bible: A Reply to a Tract Written by the Rev. J. Hay, M.A., Waltair, Madras Presidency, India*. Toronto: Baptist Publishing, 1878.

Toriani, Carlo. *History of PIME in Andhra*. Eluru, India: PIME, 2005.

Vethanayagamony, Peter. *It Began in Madras: The Eighteenth-Century Lutheran-Anglican Ecumenical Ventures in Mission and Benjamin Schultze*. Delhi: ISPCK, 2010.

Viswanath, Rupa. *The Pariah Problem: Caste, Religion, and the Social in Modern India*. New York: Columbia University Press, 2015.

Viswanathan, Gauri. *Masks of Conquest: Literary Study and British Rule in India*. New York: Columbia University Press, 1989.

Webster, John C. B. *The Dalit Christians: A History*. Delhi: ISPCK, 1992.

Whitehead, Henry. *Village Gods of South India.* New York: Oxford University Press, 1916.

Wiebe, Paul D. *Christians in Andhra Pradesh: The Mennonites of Mahbubnagar.* Madras, India: CLS, 1988.

Williams, John Bob. *A Study of the Economic Status and Self-Support of the Church of the Four Protestant Missions in the Andhra Area.* Guntur, India: Andhra Christian College, 1938.

Yagati, Chinna Rao. *Dalits' Struggle for Identity: Andhra and Hyderabad, 1900–1950.* New Delhi: Kanishka, 2003.

Zupanov, Ines G. *Disputed Mission: Jesuit Experiments and Brahmanical Knowledge in Seventeenth-Century India.* New York: Oxford University Press, 1999.

### Books in Telugu

Kalagara, Subba Rao. *Aham bahmasmi* [My self is divine]. Vijayawada, India: privately printed by Kesavarao Choudary, n.d.

———. *Yesu Prabhu! Inni thiragati tallu ekkada dhorikedhi?* [Lord Jesus! How can I find so many millstones?]. Munipalle, India: privately printed by the author, n.d.

Kalyana Rao, G. *Antarani vasantham* [Untouchable spring]. Hyderabad, India: Viplava Rachayitala Sangham, 2000.

Mangamma, J. *Andhradesamulo chraistava mishanarila seva* [Contributions of Christian missionaries to Andhra Pradesh]. Hyderabad, India: Telugu Academy, 1992.

Shyamala, Gogu. *Nallapodhu: Dalita streela sahityam* [Black dawn: Dalit women's literature]. Hyderabad, India: Hyderabad Book Trust, 2003.

Terala, Satyanarayana Sharma. *Vijayanagara Charitram: 1336–1680* [A history of Vizianagaram: 1336–1680]. Nallagonda, India: Sankranthi, 2003.

## Reports and Proceedings

*Among the Telugus: Canadian Baptist Foreign Missions Annual Report.* Toronto: Canadian Baptist Foreign Missionary Society, 1924.

*The Annual Report of the Foreign Missions of the United Lutheran Church in America.* Baltimore: BFMULCA, 1932.

*The Missionary Conference: South India and Ceylon 1879.* Vol. 2. Madras, India: Addison, 1880.

## Magazines and Journals

*Baptist Missionary Magazine.* Boston: American Baptist Missionary Union, 1871–1872.

*The Canadian Missionary Link.* Toronto: CBFMB, 1880.

*The Church Missionary Gleaner.* London: CMS, 1886.

*The Gospel Illuminator (Suvartha Prakashini).* Gunadala, India: IPC, 1974–1979.

*Lutheran Women's Work.* Philadelphia: Woman's Home and Foreign Mission Society, 1921–1923.

*The Missing Link Magazine, or Bible Work at Home and Abroad.* London: Cassell, 1871, 1872, 1877.

*The Missionary Magazine and Chronicle.* London: LMS, 1839.

## Articles in Journals

Devi, Swarnalatha. "Kavi Joshuva's Reflections on Andhra Christian Dalits." *RS* 37, no. 1 (March 1990): 35–42.

Dolbeer, Martin Luther. "The Caste Mass Movement in the Telugu Area." *NCCR* 53, no. 8 (August 1933): 420–429.

Kent, Eliza. "Tamil Bible Women and the Zenana Missions of Colonial South India." *History of Religions* 39, no. 2 (November 1999): 117–149.

Leggert, Trevor, trans. "Transmission of Buddhism to the Andhra Region." *Middle Way: Journal of the Buddhist Society* 77, no. 4 (February–April 2003): 224–225.

Lundsten, Barbara A. "The Legacy of Walter Rauschenbusch: A Life Informed by Mission." *International Bulletin of Missionary Research* 28 (April 2004): 75–78.

Nuthalapati, Evangeline Bharathi. "Women's Predicament as They Encountered Christianity: A Case Study of C.M.S. Telugu Mission in Andhra." *Indian Church History Review* 35, no. 2 (December 2001): 147–167.

Pulidindi, Solomon Raj. "Songs of the Pilgrim Churches: The Study of the Hymn Tradition of the Indigenous Mission Churches in Andhra Pradesh." *Dharma Deepika* 6, no. 1 (January–June 2002): 37–42.

Sebastian, Mrinalini. "Reading Archives from a Postcolonial Feminist Perspective: 'Native' Bible Women and the Missionary Ideal." *Journal of Feminist Studies in Religion* 19, no. 1 (Spring 2003): 5–25.

Singh, Maina C. "Women, Mission, and Medicine: Clara Swain, Anna Kugler, and Early Medical Endeavors in Colonial India." *International Bulletin of Missionary Research* 29, no. 3 (July 2005): 128–133.

Small, W. J. T. "The 'Caste' Movement in Hyderabad." *NCCR* 51, no. 2 (February 1931): 79–84.

Whittaker, Frank. "The Caste Movement towards Christianity in Northern Hyderabad." *NCCR* 53, no. 10 (October 1933): 517–531.

### Unpublished Theses and Dissertations

Injumuri, Prabhudas Asheervadam. "Dalit Conversion to the Mennonite Brethren Church in Mahabubnagar District of

Andhra Pradesh in Pre-independent India." MTh thesis, United Theological College, 1998.

———. "The Dalits' Search for Identity in the Post-independent Era: A Study of the Dalit Christian Experience in the Prakasham District of Andhra Pradesh." DTh diss., United Theological College, 2012.

Kanithi, Ranjit Kumar. "The Elements of Bhakti in the Lyrics of Acharya A. B. Masilamani: Its Implications for Mission and Its Relevance to the Convention of Baptist Churches in the Northern Circars." MTh thesis, Serampore University, 2005.

Katta, Zaccheaus. "Significance of Rituals Practiced by Hindus in CSI Medak Diocese in Andhra Pradesh." BD thesis, United Theological College, 2001.

Nuthalapati, Evangeline Bharathi. "Women in the CMS Telugu Missions, 1848–1948: Indian Women's Role and Predicament." MTh thesis, United Theological College, 2001.

### Telephone Interviews

A telephone interview with John Billa on December 12, 2020.

A telephone interview with Gabriel Chatla on September 18, 2015.

A telephone interview with John Sunder Rao on October 12, 2015.

A telephone interview with Joseph Kalyanapu on October 10, 2015.

A telephone interview with David Katuri on October 10, 2015.

A telephone interview with Prasad Kumar Marlapudi on October 1, 2015, and October 10, 2015.

A telephone interview with Vijayaratnam Nadipalli on December 10, 2015.

A telephone interview with Venkata Ratnam Sade on September 19, 2015, and November 4, 2015.

# Index